T0098324

THE PROMISE

THE PROMISE

A Tragic Accident, a Paralyzed Bride,
and the Power of Love, Loyalty, and Friendship

RACHELLE FRIEDMAN

TAYLOR TRADE PUBLISHING
Lanham • Boulder • New York • London

Published by Taylor Trade Publishing
An imprint of The Rowman & Littlefield Publishing Group, Inc.
4501 Forbes Boulevard, Suite 200, Lanham, Maryland 20706
www.rowman.com

Unit A, Whitacre Mews, 26-34 Stannary Street, London SE11 4AB

Distributed by NATIONAL BOOK NETWORK

Copyright © 2014 by Disability Possibilities, Inc.
First paperback edition 2015

All rights reserved. No part of this book may be reproduced in any form or by any electronic or mechanical means, including information storage and retrieval systems, without written permission from the publisher, except by a reviewer who may quote passages in a review.

British Library Cataloguing in Publication Information Available

Library of Congress Cataloging-in-Publication Data

The hardback edition of this book was previously catalogued by the Library of Congress as follows:

Friedman, Rachelle, author.
 The promise : a tragic accident, a paralyzed bride, and the power of love, loyalty, and friendship / Rachelle Friedman.
  p. cm.
 1. Friedman, Rachelle—Health. 2. Quadriplegics—United States—Biography.
 3. Quadriplegics—Rehabilitation—United States. 4. Friendship. 5. Biography & Autobiography / Personal Memoirs. 6. Biography & Autobiography / General.
 7. Biography & Autobiography / Women. I. Title.
  RC406.Q33 F75 2014
  362.4/3—dc23

                                                                    2014004146

ISBN 978-0-7627-9294-8 (cloth : alk. paper)
ISBN 978-1-4930-0857-5 (pbk : alk. paper)
ISBN 978-1-4930-0901-5 (electronic)

♾™ The paper used in this publication meets the minimum requirements of American National Standard for Information Sciences—Permanence of Paper for Printed Library Materials, ANSI/NISO Z39.48-1992.

Printed in the United States of America

*To anyone dealing with a spinal cord injury
and to all of those fighting tirelessly for a cure,
this book is for you.*

*To my alma mater,
East Carolina University, and the Pirate nation
for all of your support.
Once a Pirate, always a Pirate.*

Contents

When a soul is sent down from heaven it contains both male and female characteristics. The male elements enter the baby boy; the female elements enter the baby girl; and if they be worthy, God reunites them in marriage.

—THE ZOHAR

The names of all of the women by the pool the night of my accident, and of some of my friends, have been changed to protect their privacy. Some details about their identities have been slightly altered.

Prologue

My head hit the bottom of the pool and I heard an excruciatingly loud crack. Whether it was my neck snapping or my head hitting the concrete floor, I'm not really sure. I just remember that sound above all else in that moment. My eyes were open underwater, but I couldn't process what was happening. I simply floated, suspended in time. In those few seconds I didn't see a flash before my eyes. I didn't see a rush of memories. I felt frozen, as if someone had hit a pause button. I couldn't figure out anything. That crack was the only thing I heard.

When you're underwater it's usually so quiet and peaceful. But this moment didn't feel peaceful—it simply felt stuck. I felt no panic or even fear. No gasping for air and taking in water. Just my frozen mind. My body froze, too. I knew I was in water, but I couldn't feel the wetness of it; that was the strangest thing. My mind—knowing I was immersed—and my body weren't syncing up. I couldn't feel anything. I was just floating, still and nearly lifeless, toward the surface.

I had no idea when I crawled out of bed that morning that it would be the last time I'd be able to do it on my own, without help from another person. My world was about to change, as was that of my fiancé and parents.

There was another life that would unexpectedly be robbed of its joy, its ability to laugh, and it would be rocked to the core, maybe more so than mine.

CHAPTER 1

Meeting the One

OUR PLAN WAS TO HAVE EVERYTHING WE EVER WANTED: THE perfect house, a rich and happy marriage, a baby boy and a baby girl. We saw the house as the foundation of our goals and dreams. In the summer of 2009, Chris and I bought it together; it's where we were going to live our wonderfully and carefully planned life, in Knightdale, North Carolina, a small town three hours from where I grew up in Virginia Beach.

It was the Friday of my bachelorette weekend, a month before my wedding. We were home in the morning before work, scrambling to take off for fun but separate celebratory weekends. Chris was packing for his guys' camping trip. He was loading his fishing gear and clothing into the car: rods and reels, tents, all of the things you need to camp. It was all neutral colors—browns, beiges, and greens; we certainly couldn't have been packing for two more opposite events. I was preparing for a seriously girlie weekend, and he was getting ready for an ultra-guy weekend of roughing it.

My friend Britney and I had gone shopping days beforehand for a fun white dress I'd wear the next evening, and I was carefully packing my dress, curling iron, makeup, and all that I'd need to primp and party the next night. I was so worried I'd forget something, I kept reviewing what I had laid out. I was so consumed by all of the little details that were a big deal to me at the time and seemed so important. None of it turned out to be all that important in the days that followed.

Chris left before me that morning and made a point to kiss me good-bye. He was leaving for his camping trip straight from work, so I wouldn't see him until that Sunday night.

"I love you. Be safe," he said.

"I love you, too," I responded.

He went to work and so did I.

I was completely unaware it would be my last day of work ever. I was a program coordinator at an active seniors facility, and I had planned a Senior Prom for the members of the center. I dressed up in a satin polka dot dress that flared out when I twirled. I had the residents line dancing and slow dancing, and I remember dancing so hard myself. It was a fun morning. One of the couples was celebrating their fiftieth anniversary. We played a special love song for them and had them take the floor like it was their first dance. I remember looking at them and thinking, "I can't wait for this to be Chris and me." I imagined our first dance at our wedding and years of growing old together. It was a magical vision.

When I arrived home later that day, I changed out of the polka dot dress and threw on some yoga clothes for the long car ride back to my hometown. Britney picked me up that afternoon. When I left our beautiful home on May 21, 2010, I left a few dishes in the sink, the bed unmade, and a bunch of outfits on the floor that I had torn out of my closet to pack and never put back. I figured I'd clean up when I returned home. I was too excited to waste time. I had set my bag right at the door, so I could just zip in and grab it after work.

Britney and I headed to my grandma's house for our big Saturday. It's the place I always go when I head to my hometown. It's easier there. My room at my mom and dad's had been turned into a storage office, but my grandma had a real room for me still, so I liked it there. I was celebrating with my girls; Chris was celebrating with his dad. Soon, we'd be husband and wife, a day I'd waited for my entire life.

Chris and I met at East Carolina University in Greenville at a party in 2004, during my freshman year. It was October, and Halloween was a serious weeklong affair there. In fact, it's apparently one of the biggest Hallows' Eve celebrations in the country, almost like a mini Mardi Gras. This was a Friday night, October 29. But two days later, on Halloween night, all the streets would be full of people shoulder to shoulder.

It was an outdoor party, part of the festivities that we'd heard about through the grapevine. None of my dorm mates in Tyler Hall knew the guys hosting it, but we had heard it would be fun. We all got ready together, trying on a bunch of different outfits, clothes scattered everywhere. I settled on light capri jeans, a brown silky halter top, and some dangly turquoise earrings. I had my hair pulled sort of halfway back, so that you could see my jewelry.

My roommate, two other girls, and I set out in the early evening to find the place, which was all the way across campus, but we made a stop along the way. The main part of campus was designed like a square, with everything essentially no more than one mile away. I lived on College Hill, across from the main campus. We stopped at a guy friend's place first, and we began playing beer pong. With a few more people in our crowd, we headed to the party, located close to downtown Greenville. We knew we were getting close as we walked, because we could hear the din of the party blocks away. It was one loud constant noise. We walked around to the backyard, which was full of people—every square inch covered. This was by far the biggest party I'd ever attended.

My friends and I edged our way through the crowd and found our way into the house; we bought vodka and orange juice drinks before heading back outside. I saw this guy Mike that my roommate had already met, and we were all introduced to his two roommates, Chris and Tom. I thought Mike was really cute when I saw him standing there. My roommate Mary was interested in Mike, too.

I kind of flirted with all three of them that night. I was a flirtatious girl then, and it was fun to have that attention. We were all chatting and laughing over drinks. Mike, it turned out, was Chris's cousin and roommate, and as we were all standing there talking, I couldn't stop thinking about how cute he was. I didn't notice Chris as much, because I was so drawn to Mike initially. I was talking to the group of them really, not just one person. We talked for a while, getting bumped around by passing partygoers. Mike headed through the crowds with my roommate, so they could chat with some other people. I wound up sort of isolated, alone with just Chris at that point. Since the music was playing and I loved randomly teaching people to salsa dance, I grabbed Chris's hand.

"C'mon, let's dance. I'll show you how."

He was totally up for it. It was crowded, so we were moving in a tiny space as we danced.

"Where are you from?" I asked.

"Virginia Beach," he said.

"Me, too!"

I had been drinking and, after a couple of songs, took a break. I turned to him and said, "So, where are you from?"

He answered again. We laugh about this, but I asked him twice more that night. He finally said, "The same place you are from!"

Chris and Tom and I all left the party together at the end of the night. Although our other friends headed straight back to Mike's place, we went to Alfredo's to get pizza. There was a standing joke in Greenville that the pizza was edible at this place only if you had been drinking. We waited for what seemed like an hour for our pizza, then headed back to Mike's to hang out for a few more hours, all of us just talking and laughing about the night. This was my freshman year, and looking back I realize that it was the most important night of my life.

Like many of those college crushes, my roommate was over Mike by sunrise. He must have done something to turn her off. Back in our dorm I asked her, "Do you mind if I go for Mike?"

"Go for it," she said.

We hung out again on Halloween, two nights later. Mike and I were flirting with each other and even holding hands, but it didn't go anywhere beyond that night.

But by December that year, Chris and I were buddies. I had a lot of guy friends then, so I didn't think much of it. We were both going home for the holidays, and he offered to give me a ride. He picked me up in his Buick Le Sabre. We lived about two and a half hours away from school, both from the same town (as we'd by now laughed about many times). We talked about a lot of things on that drive, but honestly, since I wasn't even remotely thinking about him romantically, I don't remember much of the discussion.

To me, it was just a ride home. But I do recall that he implied he was having problems with his girlfriend, that things hadn't really been the same with the two of them. I wasn't in a place to give advice, since I hadn't ever been in a serious relationship in my life. He said that he was looking forward to a week apart from her to think things through. The term "breakup" wasn't a part of our conversation, but he suggested they'd assess things when they returned to school in the New Year. I may not have known much about relationships, but I could tell he wasn't happy. As his friend, happiness was all I wanted for him.

While I didn't have those kinds of special feelings about Chris, I was struck immediately by the fact that he was a really awesome, stand-up guy. It was something you could just tell, especially as we rode together that day and I listened to him talk. It sounds so corny and general, but it became obvious to me that Chris was a crazily honest and extremely genuine person. I could tell from the very beginning that he would never intentionally hurt someone, or purposely lie or be mean. He was just always so nice.

He took me to my house, and that's when we figured out how close we lived to each other. I knew he was in Virginia Beach, but I had never bothered to ask him where exactly. So when I gave him directions to my grandmother's house, we were shocked that his home was literally in the same neighborhood, and we could have walked to each other's houses. We did learn that our paths had crossed before college. We had the same dentist—my uncle. Chris had been to my dad's army-navy surplus store, too. Basically, he'd met several members of my family before ever meeting me. I used to go to the pool in the community when I was little, in the summers, and he said he was there every day for years, as was I, starting at age three. Chris was four years older than me, a big difference then. We're not sure if we played together, but we might have. Virginia Beach is not a small place. It's not a big city, but it's spread out, so to discover we'd been in the same neighborhood was pretty crazy.

He helped me bring my stuff inside and met my grandma for the first time, and she'll tell you to this day that she never saw me look at a guy like that before, that she saw our future right there. She saw it well before I did. I didn't see that at all.

CHAPTER 2

From Friend to Soul Mate

I JUMPED OUT OF BED THE NEXT MORNING, SO EXCITED THINKING about the bachelorette day ahead. My friend Britney had stayed overnight with me at my grandma's house in Virginia Beach. It was like a sleepover. We stayed in one room, and my grandma made us my favorite breakfast that morning: pancakes and scrambled eggs.

There was so much to do. My day was jam-packed with plans and appointments and last-minute shopping. I was getting my final fitting for my wedding dress; having lunch with my mom, Bubbie (my dad's mom), and Britney; and then heading off to celebrate my pending wedding with my other friends. Lauren was still making her way to town, and the other girls were busy prepping and planning the night ahead, so they didn't join us for lunch. It was my bachelorette party. I was going to marry my Prince Charming, the man of my dreams: Chris Chapman. This day was all part of the celebration leading up to that.

I was excited to hang out with this group of girls because we would all be going out together for the first time. They knew of each other, but we hadn't spent too much time together as a group before. Lauren, Samantha, Carly, and Britney—all from different periods of my life—would finally really get to know each other and spend time together to celebrate with me. Just the five of us. But before the evening's festivities, the group from lunch went to the bridal shop, so that I could try on my wedding dress for the very last fitting.

I had gone shopping for my wedding dress two weeks after I got engaged. All the girls were there, and each one went and grabbed a dress off the rack. Lauren pulled the one I ultimately chose. It was just beautiful. I tried on only four, but I fell in love with that one immediately. It was a strapless dress, corseted at the top and laced down the back. The skirt flowed from there, and it had an incredible train. My mom had seen it when I first picked it out, but when she looked at me in it all fitted and ready to wear, she was overjoyed. She said it looked like it was made just for me. She had wanted to buy it for me and I accepted, knowing how happy it made her to do that, even though she'd have to work very hard to do so. Everyone thought it was beautiful.

The bridal shop finished some of the alterations, and then we all headed out for a quick lunch at Applebee's in town. I brought my veil and some flowers with me. After lunch we went to a local hair salon for a trial on how I'd wear my hair on my wedding day. We tried updos and all down, but in the end, we decided that curls, with half pulled up along the sides, would be best. I left with that look, which was great because I'd wear it out for the party that evening.

The biggest stress of the day was finding the right shoes for the bachelorette night. I wanted the perfect white high heels, or else I felt like the entire outfit would be ruined. I was sort of frantic that I wouldn't find what I had in mind: really high stilettos, strappy and white, of course. I wound up finding the perfect pair, not knowing that even the ideal shoes couldn't change the outcome of the night.

***

Chris and I had made it through the entire spring semester in 2005 without dating, but our friendship had grown really deep. He had become my very best friend. His relationship with his girlfriend had withered by then, and by April they'd broken up. He and I spent a lot of time together, but I didn't think anything of it beyond us being friends.

In early June of that year, he invited me to his family's vacation house on Lake Gaston by myself. We were just friends, but I knew at this point that he liked me. It was a little awkward, but I wanted to go because I thought it would be fun, and it was not too weird because we had been hanging out all of the time. I remember it was really hot around that time. I was wearing a little red bikini, sunbathing on the dock, which was down a hill a bit from the house. It was over water, connecting the house to the boathouse. The main house was a rustic place—wood, painted brown, not stained. It was on a street called Happy Valley, which was fitting because it was a really happy place. It was one of the original houses built on the lake. Chris's grandfather had built it with his bare hands, and Chris's dad had grown up spending summers at the lake house.

They had two rules at the house: You could have anything you wanted, but you had to get it yourself, and there was no skinny-dipping before ten o'clock at night. It was sweet because this house, which had sort of a main section and then some other newer additions, was a throwback surrounded by other large modern houses that were built later. It sat on a little cove, overlooking the main lake. The streets were eventually all paved, but leading up to the house was a long, straight gravel drive. You could smell the water and hear the ripples lapping up against the dock. I later learned that as I lay there that day, listening to the peaceful sound of the water, Chris was checking me out from the back deck as I caught some sun in my little bikini. I wasn't trying to taunt him, but I guess I should have known that wearing a red string bikini in front of a guy with a crush wasn't entirely innocent.

I was still wearing that same bikini when we went out on their boat that afternoon, and that's when Chris shifted his approach from staring from afar to pursuing me. We were on the boat on the lake, and he let me drive. He sat behind me and helped me steer. I'd never driven a boat before, and it was calming to have him guiding me. It felt protective and sweet. He was getting closer to me than maybe he ever had before, and then he set his hand on my thigh. It wasn't completely smooth or subtle, but it wasn't overt, either; he wasn't rubbing it in a sexual way, but it was for sure not the way a friend would touch another friend. I didn't know how to react. It was how a boy touched a girl, and I felt panicked. He left his hand on my leg for a long time; that's how I knew. It was clearly flirtatious, but all new to me.

A couple of weekends later, a group of us went to the lake, including his cousin and some of our other friends. He decided to take me for a walk around the streets in the lake neighborhood, just the two of us, and I remember him holding my hand. It was completely foreign to me, and I was so nervous. I had held a guy's hand before, but not like this, not so tenderly, and definitely not in a situation like this one that was brewing with feelings. I didn't know what it meant or what to do about it, other than to simply hold it back. I liked it, I guess. It felt natural and fun to be holding his hand.

I was wearing a bathing suit, board shorts, and a T-shirt. I hadn't gotten extra dolled up or anything; I was just wearing what I normally wore in the summer. I grew up at the beach, so I was always wearing bikinis. The walk was definitely awkward, but I think I picked up on his motives and panicked just a bit again.

"Everyone we know is in a relationship that sucks, don't you think?" I blurted out for no reason other than nerves. I was thinking things and just saying them without censoring myself at all.

"I guess," he said.

"It scares me. I don't really see many relationships going so well. And then when these people all break up, what's left? They can't even be friends anymore. It makes you really think, you know?"

"Yeah," he said.

This guy had basically taken me on a walk to ask me out, and here I was talking about these horrible relationships and how I was scared of them.

We were nearly ending our walk and almost back at his house when he finally found the courage to ask me the question he'd been saving. We stopped halfway up the driveway, and he asked, "Do you see yourself in a relationship ever?"

I was honest. I said, "Yeah." That's it. That's all I said.

Then he grew a little braver and asked, "Do you see yourself in a relationship with me?" He said it like it was an official question that he'd been working on for a while. He didn't ask me out exactly, just inquired about our potential future.

I said, "Yes." I paused for just a second and said, "But I'm really scared." By then my head was spinning. We continued walking at that point, and my head swirled with fear. We were roommates at college for the summer and we were best friends. I didn't want to give up either of those things. I kept thinking, *What if it doesn't work out?* When we walked around the house on the deck, everyone was hanging out, and I knew we needed more time to talk.

We stole a few more minutes away from the crowd by continuing past them all and slipping onto the back part of the deck for privacy. I tried to explain myself, but I just started talking in circles. I told him I was confused, and he said he could tell. I then took my second "yes" back in a way. I could feel myself breaking his heart, but I couldn't stop rambling about my fears.

"I don't know right now. But that doesn't mean never," I said. "I'm just scared right now."

He didn't say anything. He leaned down and kissed my forehead.

I spent the rest of the evening wishing I could take back all of my babbling. What Chris had done, what he had said, was the sweetest gesture ever. But there were so many people around, and I was too afraid of everything happening so quickly.

That night, we actually shared a bed. We didn't cuddle or do anything at all; the house was so full of people, and it seemed the obvious plan that we would bunk together. All night I thought about what he had said and the kiss on my forehead.

We wound up being separated that next week, so my fear and what he had said just lingered, unresolved. I returned to Greenville, and he went to Raleigh to see his cousin Mike. While Chris was there Mike called and told me that he had a friend that he thought would really hit it off with me, that we would be a good match. Worse, there was another girl at the house with them that Mike wanted to set Chris up with. I thought, *I've blown it all with Chris.*

It was an awful week. I was afraid of moving forward with Chris, but then I was suddenly scared of losing him, too. And I was jealous at the same time, which really surprised me. That was a big realization for me. It didn't change the terror of being nineteen years old and realizing that maybe I was falling for my future husband, or worrying that I'd fallen for my best friend but would lose both him and his friendship in the end. It was a weird pull, balancing commitment with potential for loss. It was an indescribable tug of war inside of me.

At some point midweek I took Tom aside in his room to help me sort things out in my head. He was also our summer roommate, and so he'd seen the progression of things.

"I don't know what to do," I said.

"I think you should just do it, go for it," he said.

"I know. I'm nervous, though."

"Chris could be your future husband," he said. He was half joking, I think.

"Don't say that. You're freaking me out!"

"He could be, though," he said.

"I know. But it scares me."

Ultimately, when I thought it through, I realized it was almost inevitable we'd at least give it a go and try to be together, mainly because besides fear, I couldn't make the argument for not being with Chris. He was a perfect guy. He was honest and genuine, we got along, and we both liked the same things—going out, outdoor stuff, and travel. We were both ECU Pirates fans, which was important. We had everything in common, but I had never had a boyfriend, I didn't know how this was all supposed to work, and I didn't want the good stuff to end if the romance fizzled.

The bigger fear, of course, was that I'd messed it all up and it was too late. That I'd let this great guy slip on by.

CHAPTER 3

The Bachelorette Party

AFTER MY HAIR WAS SET AND MY PERFECT SHOES PURCHASED, Britney and I headed over to Carly's house for the evening festivities, but I had to wait in the car for a few minutes because apparently the girls were still decorating outside. I was thrilled to be having a bachelorette party in my honor. This was one of those things we all thought about as a teen—part of the entire wedding celebration—and it was with friends I really enjoyed being around.

It was early, around five o'clock or so, and the weather was perfect, with that late spring smell in the air, when you know summer and all its excitement are fast approaching. I was wearing the casual clothes I'd had lunch in, but I had the great dress with me to change into for later that night—white, like the one I'd wear on my wedding day. But this one was fun, cute, and short. I was giddy. The four girls—Carly, Lauren, Britney, and Samantha—were going to wear a shade of purple, just like they'd wear for the wedding. Purple was one of my school colors and my favorite color, too.

All of these girls were from such different walks of my life. Lauren was my oldest friend. We'd met when we were two years old, when our brothers were in Boy Scouts together. She was the sister I never had. She lived in Charlotte now, but she was the kind of friend where no matter how much time had passed, it didn't matter; we picked up right where we had left off. We used to make videos together of us dancing and acting silly. Her mom had a whole stack of VHS tapes of us. We took acting lessons together and used to make big plans to live on a farm with a bunch of horses.

Carly and I met in middle school when I was twelve. She ended up going to a different high school, but we stayed friends. We loved to sing together. Carly was a phenomenal musician, great at both piano and guitar. We loved showing off by putting shows on for our friends.

I met Samantha through Carly in freshman year of high school, when Carly brought me to a birthday party. Samantha and I didn't get along right away. She thought I was a dork, and I thought she was a snob. We both judged too quickly. We slowly warmed up to each other and grew closer over the summer. I got to know her really well when we worked together at the beach. We used to have so much fun. Our one job was basically to sit there, a little ways apart from each other on the beach, and wait for people to come and rent stuff from us. We each had our own station, and although we stayed extremely busy, it was still boring work. Sometimes we would sneak away and go bodyboarding for a few minutes in the middle of our shift to break up the monotony. Of course, we'd return to shambles—people using umbrellas they hadn't paid for and such—and we'd have to backtrack to make up for the time. To liven it all up, we made a book. We were just far enough apart that we couldn't sit and talk to each other. So we made this book and we'd write funny things in it—well, things that we thought were funny—and then we'd run it back and forth across the sand. That's how we communicated all day.

We would write things like how cute some of the beach boys were. We talked about going dancing. We were both dancing queens and we'd turned eighteen around the same time, so we could finally go dancing at the clubs downtown at night. Our senior year we went out all the time together on weekends.

So all of the other lifeguards knew about the book and they wanted it. I remember one asking, "What's in the book?"

As he was asking I wrote his name in it, big so he could see. Then he kept asking if he could see it. It was fun. It kept us entertained as we sat under an umbrella in a beach chair all day.

Britney and I met in 2009. Her boyfriend and Chris had played ball at the university together. We were in the clubhouse playing pool one night right after college, both living in the same apartment complex. She and her boyfriend had recently graduated, too. It was practically the first week out of school for all of us. Chris and her boyfriend bumped into each other and introduced us. It was a quick encounter and I didn't think much of it at the time, nor did she obviously, as we didn't say much more than hello to each other. A week later, I saw a girl washing "Go ECU!" paint off the side of her car. Drawn to a fellow Pirate fan, I approached, hoping to make a new friend. I began talking and then a minute in, I realized it was Britney. After that we kept bumping into each other. We'd go to each other's apartments and out in downtown Raleigh frequently. It was so nice to have a girlfriend close by.

Britney wasn't in the bridal party, but she was joining our celebration. There were a few more girls who were supposed to come out with us, but they wound up not being able to make it that night, so it was just the five of us. At the time, Britney wasn't a bridesmaid because another friend of mine, Sandra, was in the wedding. But that friend and I had drifted apart, and I wished I could have had Britney in my wedding party because we'd grown so close. Unfortunately, we couldn't get another dress to match, and I couldn't very well ask the other friend to step aside and give up her dress for no reason.

When they finally let me in that night at Carly's, I felt so happy to be with them. They had hung pink banners everywhere and decorated outside beautifully. They were excited to surprise me with the decorations. The patio looked nice, all done up. We sat under an umbrella around a table catching up, enjoying the weather. We grilled some burgers and hot dogs and had a little bit of champagne to kick off the night. The limo would arrive much later to take us dancing. The girls had set up games on the deck, some of them too racy to mention, but ultimately we never played any of them, because we all talked too much.

Britney had us in hysterics. She was telling us all how she couldn't go to the bathroom anywhere other than at home, no matter where she was—it was a genuine phobia. She relayed a story about how she went on vacation with her boyfriend for the first time to his family's house, and it was small and she just couldn't relieve herself. She was afraid of people hearing it. She's always had to jump through hoops to avoid using public restrooms, so she often made us laugh with her extraordinary stories.

At some point in the evening, just for a few minutes, my parents stopped by to give me a hug and say hello. It was a very significant hug, though none of us had any idea how significant. It would be the last time they'd see me stand . . . or give me a hug at eye level.

After dinner I was sitting on Lauren's lap, reminiscing.

"How crazy is it that we were just Girl Scouts, like yesterday, playing softball and basketball together, and now we're getting married within a month of each other?" she asked.

"I know. Soon, we'll both be married old ladies," I replied.

"But it's cool how our lives have always been parallel for so long. We even used to have joint birthday parties together! Now basically weddings, too."

As we toasted, clinking glasses, I thought about how lucky I was to have such awesome friends to celebrate with, and I was really looking forward to the rest of the evening. We all got along that night, and it was one of those rare times when everyone just became fast friends. It was almost an instant connection. I had no way of knowing as we talked exactly how important and significant that group friendship was about to become. We discussed the fact that it was actually kind of unusual that we all got along so well, with only me as the common thread. Someone made the point that everyone was so welcoming and how rare that was these days. In an eerie way, even before an unspoken bond was formed, the promise of continued friendship was apparent. This was a good group of people, period.

In 2002, in tenth grade at my private school, I joined the varsity cheerleading squad. The girls on the team did not like me because I wasn't Miss Popular. They would leave me out of everything, including dinners before games. I'd remain at school the entire time in between practice and the start of a game, because I couldn't drive yet. I remember feeling restricted and stuck. Rarely did someone step up and be mean to my face, but behind my back they were awful. The other cheerleaders were always whispering about me, which made it hard for me to defend myself. Looking back now, I really wish I had stood up to them. I did prevail in a sense, though, because that year I was awarded MVP cheerleader, and man, were they pissed. No one said congrats. When I heard my name announced, I felt that all of the tears they'd caused me were worth it. I wasn't brave enough to stand up for myself back then.

That was the same summer I started working at the beach with some friends, renting out umbrellas. We were such beach bums and would go bodyboarding for hours. We partied with the lifeguards every week, but the most I ever drank was three or four Mike's Hard Lemonades. That was when I first tried alcohol. I was actually kind of a goody-goody, and I think it annoyed my friends at school, but these girls didn't care.

I really came out of my shell around then. I'm not sure what changed, but for the first time I felt beautiful, sexy, fun, and popular. I wished I could have felt like that at school, but around the girls there I never really did. It took meeting people like Carly and Samantha to remind me of how friendships were supposed to be, how people were supposed to treat each other. By senior year I had decided to change high schools and graduate elsewhere, because I didn't want to deal with the drama anymore at the private school.

After dinner and a lot of laughter, we all dolled ourselves up, ready to hit the clubs. It was about eight o'clock, and we were excited to go out dancing. I felt like I was in my college dorm room, all of us in one bathroom, giggling and applying our makeup, cracking jokes about how nicely we had cleaned up. I wore my white satin dress, and they all slipped on their various shades of purple and matching black belts. My favorite dance music was Britney Spears, so as a treat Samantha created a really cool mix of all of her songs, which we planned to blare in the limo.

After about an hour we started taking pictures. Carly's mom took pictures of the group of us, and we laughed the entire time. The limo was picking us up at ten. Just before we were leaving, we went down to the kitchen and mixed up this crazy red drink concoction to take with us while we headed from club to club. A black stretch limo pulled up in front of the house, and we jumped in with our red drinks, ready for a fun night. At one point while we were driving around, I managed to spill the red drink on my white dress. Of course, I was the only one spilling and the only one in white, so it couldn't have felt more disastrous at the time. As I sat there soaked down the front and about to freak out, Lauren yelled up to the driver, "Stop at the next Rite Aid you see."

Within a couple of minutes, he pulled over. Britney and Lauren ran inside, bought five bleach pens, and went to town on the dress. After about ten minutes of intense scrubbing and rubbing, we all looked down and agreed the cleanup had worked. Tragedy had been averted. Later, looking at the dress in the light, I could see that it was still totally stained. I had a pink sash on that said

"Bachelorette," so maybe that hid it or helped it blend a little. And ultimately it didn't matter at all.

We went to clubs all over town, and it was so cool pulling up in a limo. We stepped out like we were total rock stars. It was an incredible feeling, being treated to such a decadent night with such great people. But I wasn't quite graceful enough to live up to my pretend status. At the second club everyone poured out of the car. We headed up to the second floor, making our way to the upper deck. We reached the top, and everyone looked our way to acknowledge that a bachelorette party had arrived. Right in that moment, the heel of my shoe got stuck between the wooden deck boards. My shoe stayed, I didn't, and I fell almost facedown, sprawled out in front of everyone in line. We all thought it was the most hilarious thing that ever could have happened, and we laughed about it as they helped me up. I cheered loudly with them to play it off as cool as possible.

We danced all night, and at one o'clock in the morning, we climbed into the limo to head back home. We had to carry our shoes at this point, because our feet were so sore from the high heels. We had been drinking, but we weren't really drunk. We were sober enough to know when to go home. I've thought a lot about the timing of this night and wondered how it could have gone differently. If I *had* gotten drunk, would I have gone right to sleep when I got back to Carly's house? If we'd gone to one more club, would we have been too tired for the next series of events? I've thought about how and when we decided to call the night and head home and how that timing determined the outcome of the rest of my life.

CHAPTER 4

The Accident

LAUREN AND I USED TO DREAM OF BEING MERMAIDS WHEN WE were little and argue over who got to be Ariel. Every Sunday, my dad, Larry, used to take me to a cafeteria for breakfast where they had a fountain. I'd always ask for two pennies to make a wish. I'd use one to wish I was a mermaid, but because I felt that was a selfish wish, I always used the second penny to wish for world peace.

Once we were all danced out, Lauren suggested we take a swim when we returned to Carly's house. We all raced out of the limo and ran upstairs to change into our bathing suits. The night had been so much fun. We had talked a lot about Chris and our future and boys they liked, too. These girls had heard it all before, but part of the fun of the night was getting all the attention as a bride-to-be, and we talked about not only how Chris and I ultimately got together after all my crazy fears but also how we almost didn't.

$\sim$

During that week when Chris and I were apart, before we became a couple, all I could think about was how I wanted to take back everything I had said. I wanted to replace "No, I don't want to date you" with "Oh, I've changed my mind because there is this new girl coming along for you and I don't want to miss out on the greatest thing ever." But I just couldn't yet.

The girl and the guy that Mike had planned for us both did visit, but nothing came of it for either me or Chris. Thankfully. Finally, after that week of being apart, we both wound up at Virginia Beach, and that entire time I could think of nothing else but Chris and our future together. I even had trouble sleeping. I was obsessed with figuring out what my feelings meant and why I had him on my mind.

I would think over and over again in my head, *What do I do? What do I do?* I couldn't focus on anything else. That's when it became obvious that we had to remain good friends *and* become a couple. Both were allowed. Both could work. It took me some time to figure out that we could do both, but when I did I knew I'd had a life-altering epiphany. Embracing one didn't mean giving up the other. I think I knew, or at least hoped, that it was going to work out and that ultimately I wouldn't have to sacrifice friendship for love, because we would survive on both levels. I felt it in my gut, and the decision felt peaceful and right.

We arranged to meet, and he picked me up at midnight and then we drove to the oceanfront. We wound up at 65th Street, and we sat on the beach cuddling. I was kind of clingy with him because I hadn't seen him, and I remember thinking, *I am just going to have to ask him because he's definitely not going to re-ask me.*

We were sitting there alone, with a bright moon lighting up the beach, and I said, "We need to talk."

I am pretty sure a guy never wants to hear those words, but I said them anyway. He looked worried, that much I could tell.

Still, I looked at him and said, "I thought about it a lot this week, and I'm ready for us to move forward. I want to be with you."

"Are you sure?" he asked.

I nodded and said, "Yes."

We didn't even kiss—we just lay there hugging, embracing, and sitting intertwined on the beach all night long. It might sound like a made-for-the-movies scene from a fairy tale love story, but we saw the sunrise together. It was just awesome.

At the crack of dawn, we were still laughing and talking. We hadn't slept at all, and we were giddy. We got up when it became light, and we ran around a bit on the beach. He picked me up and spun me around, and I remember thinking it was the greatest moment. It had been a perfect night. That night we named the street leading to the spot on the beach *our street*.

I had never dated anyone, and I was glad we had eliminated all the pressure of a date, not knowing what each of us was feeling. There were no games or manipulation. We just decided to be each other's. We wanted to belong to each other, and we said so without any hesitation. I don't know what it feels like to meet a guy with the hope and intention that it turns into something; to be friends and already know each other on that level, and to have it gradually develop, felt natural. I had this feeling right then, as we were watching the sun and horsing around, that once we committed to each other it would never end. I was a good judge of character, and after knowing Chris for eight months, it seemed like he was flawless and we meshed so well together. I felt I was giving in to a perfect connection that no one I knew had ever had, and it seemed like I was starting my forever.

The summer we started dating was the best summer ever because he didn't have a job and I quit my job at a camping and

cycling store. I was really good at ringing people up, but I didn't know any details about road bikes, and it was hard to learn. Once I gave my notice, then Chris and I could do whatever we wanted. Fortunately, I had a little financial help from my parents, though my expenses totaled less than two hundred dollars per month. Still, that freedom made it possible for us to have a blast. We would stay up until five in the morning talking and just being together. We would sleep in, get up and eat, and then go out at night with our friends. We'd go to the lake all the time and ride around on the boat and go wakeboarding. We had this one Rascal Flatts CD, and it was the anthem of the summer. During the week in Greenville, we would always go out in big groups, but Chris and I would slip away on the weekends and go sunbathing and swimming and just be together. It was unbreakable, our bond. I think that bond made what happened by the pool that night, knowing we were together forever, manageable.

⌐ ⌐

I went outside to the pool with the girls, but I was being kind of a wimp about going in because of the temperature. It had cooled off slightly, and in a bathing suit, I was making a little noise about going in the water. It was dark, with only the moon lighting the deck and the water. We were all in a really good mood and still laughing as much as we had been when the night first began.

No one else had even gone in the water yet. The voices—who was saying what, who was giggling, who was standing where—all blurred together.

Suddenly, I felt two cold hands on my back, and then a little playful push sent me into the water.

Two feet to the right, and I would have been in the deep end. Two feet to the right, and I would still be walking. Two feet changed the course of my life forever. That's it. Two feet.

I don't know why, but when I felt the hands on my back giving me a light, fun shove, instead of just falling, my reflex was to dive in. Head first instead of feet first. But my arms weren't locked out enough, so they weakened, and I hit my head on the bottom of the pool. In a split second everything froze. My mind, my body. I was in complete shock. I floated up to the top, facedown in the water, like a lifeless body, bobbing. Suddenly, I was on my back, my face out of the water, allowing me to gasp once for air and then yell, "Help." I thought I had floated onto my back myself, but since I couldn't feel anything, I didn't know someone had turned me over in the water after jumping in to get me. I looked up and said, "This isn't a joke—y'all need to call 911." Ironically, almost all of us had worked as lifeguards. A couple of other people jumped in as well, and I remember Samantha tried to do the correct thing by stabilizing me in the water until EMS arrived. I was so cold and scared that I just looked at her and said, "Get me the fuck out of the water." I later learned it wasn't the impact as much as the angle that caused my injury. It really could have been much worse. My arms may not have locked, but ultimately, my hands protected my head when it hit. There could have been substantially more damage had this not been the case.

I was a lifeguard, too, and I should have known better than to tell them to get me out of the water. Ultimately, I'm not sure if it made a difference or not. They all helped pull me out and put me on the side of the pool, with my lower legs dangling in the water.

My first moment of true fear was looking down at my legs, seeing them in the water but not being able to feel all of the sensations associated with water. I couldn't feel anything.

I knew it was serious as I lay there.

Before help arrived someone was holding my hand. I was just staring into her eyes as we waited.

"I can't feel my legs. Something isn't right," I said.

"It's probably just some kind of nerve damage; don't worry," someone said calmly. "It's not serious, I'm sure."

Everything was sort of foggy at this point. My friends remained by my side. What I remember clearly was the reaction of my friend who had playfully pushed me. She kept apologizing. In that moment I knew she would carry a huge amount of guilt, and I didn't want her to live with that. I told her right there, as I was waiting for EMS to arrive, that it would be okay. I comforted her even though I was scared myself. Even in that moment, I knew it was important to do so.

It was right then under the moonlight, after my wonderful bachelorette party, that a silent pact was formed, though in the coming months it would become formalized. It was a chilling event that changed all of our lives: the innocence we were experiencing that night at the pool, and then robbed of, and the moments of scramble to save me. It was there as I was lying at the side of the pool that instantly we all bonded. Despite the reason for our bond, it became the strongest force in my life, next to my love for Chris. If I hadn't met this group of girls, and had instead been surrounded by some of the mean ones I went to high school with, I'm not sure I'd have survived the hurdles I dealt with in the wake of that night. These friendships saved me. Most girls are competitive with each other. Not this group. We redefined friendship that night and built a support system so strong even tragedy couldn't break it.

None of us has ever revealed the name of the girl who playfully pushed me that night, and none of us ever will. Protecting her has always been too important, her feelings too important, the situation too fragile and fraught with potential pain. Besides, it could have been any one of us. Any one of our lives could have been impacted by one playful gesture. Any one of us could have lived with that guilt forever. Any one of us could have been pulled motionless from the chilly water. I think as we waited for help, we all knew the tables easily could have been turned. We'd all played by the pool before and we all knew that what happened to me, what happened to her, could have happened to any of us. For that reason, the name of that one girl who maybe suffered most in all of this remained at the side of the pool that night. That secret will stay with all of us forever.

CHAPTER 5

Paralyzed

THE EMERGENCY MEDICAL WORKERS ARRIVED AND CHECKED MY vitals, then prepared to hustle me into the ambulance.

"What's wrong?" I asked.

"You likely have a broken neck," one said.

I thought, *Holy crap, I just broke my neck and lived.* Then I said, "Whoa, I'm a badass."

Despite my joking, I was concerned my condition was most likely permanent. I looked at one of the EMS workers and asked, "How many people in your experience have walked away from something like this?"

She didn't answer right away. They both just kept working. I said, "Don't beat around the bush. Tell me."

The EMS worker said, "In my thirty years on the job, only one person has walked away."

I looked at her and said, "Well, I'll be the second." Maybe it was false hope I was grasping on to, but hey, it got me through those next few hours.

They placed me in the back of the ambulance; the trip from the pool to the vehicle was a blur. Lauren ran alongside as they moved me and jumped into the front seat of the ambulance to make the trip to the hospital. She told me later that the driver was a guy she went to church with as a child and hadn't seen since then. In all the hustle, they didn't notice until they were driving away toward the hospital.

Before I knew it I was on my back on a metal table in the hospital in Virginia Beach with my neck being stabilized. The room was small and bright. Saying it was *like a dream* sounds cliché, but it felt unreal, like it couldn't possibly be happening to me. I felt like I was witnessing someone else's horror, not experiencing my own. It took all of my energy to remain calm.

I asked anyone who came in, "What's happening?" and "What are you not telling me?" I couldn't really get any answers. Every nurse and doctor who came in said, "Let's wait for your neurologist." Until he arrived, no one was telling me anything.

The girls were in the waiting room, and my parents had been called. They got to the hospital before I did and were with me the entire time. My grandparents and Chris's mom, Susan, all arrived at some point, but Chris wasn't there. He was out of town on his camping trip and couldn't be reached right away. He was camping with his dad at Eno River State Park in Durham, about three hours away. He told me later that the park rangers found them and said only that there was a big family emergency. They both thought Chris's ninety-year-old grandmother, who had been suffering from Alzheimer's, had passed away. They finally found a point with cell reception, and his dad called home. Chris heard him say, "I understand." Then he hung up the phone.

He said to Chris, "Are you settled and okay?"

Chris said, "Yes."

His dad said, "Well, you're not about to be."

His dad drove him back to our house in Knightdale, and he raced in to grab clothes and dump the camping gear. His father told him only that there had been an accident and that I had been hurt. They both knew it was bad, but not exactly how bad. He said later that he took a very quick shower because they had been roughing it, and he cried so hard in the shower that he could hardly see.

My parents never left my side in the examining room, trying to be comforting, stroking my hair as we waited. I think it was tough on the people working there, because I was young and otherwise vibrant. Someone told me later that my makeup was basically still on, that it looked almost perfect, and that my hair had dried in pretty blond waves. I think that image of a young girl made it even harder on them. I learned later that one of the EMS volunteers who had taken me to the hospital made mine her last call because it was just too upsetting for her to process, and she didn't want to encounter anything so tragic again.

I was calm, I really was. Maybe calmer than everyone else who was there. But I guess I knew things were dire by their demeanors and worried looks, and I just wanted the facts, not the pity. Everyone's fears were evident. My one panic was Chris. I desperately wanted to talk to him, to tell him I was going to be okay. I was certain he was beside himself without details. All I knew, after a few hours, was that they'd finally located him and his father.

I had to have CAT scans and MRIs and no one was allowed to accompany me, but since my mom's brother Steve worked at the hospital, he was able to be with me and actually perform the scans. It was nice to have him there while everyone waited.

Eventually, after the tests were completed and my parents had rejoined me, the neurologist came in. It was his first time in the ER.

"Why does he look so scared?" I asked. The nurse made up a reason about something else happening in the hospital. He was touching me all over.

"Can you feel that?" he asked.

"Can you feel that?" Again.

"That?"

I couldn't feel any of it. And he was just asking, not giving me any information. It was excruciating for us all as he did the test.

After a few minutes he stopped the test and said plainly, "You will never walk again."

My parents were the only other people in the room at the time, and they broke down crying and held each other.

"What are the chances that she might?" my dad asked.

"Maybe five percent?" the doctor replied.

My parents sobbed. It was heartbreaking to hear them in tears and in such pain. I felt worse for them, actually, than I did for me. I was in shock, I guess, but the implications of what it meant for me just felt far less than what it meant for everyone else I loved. I watched them cry, and my heart sank. I kept thinking over and over in my head, *You will get through this. Stay strong. It's going to be okay.* One at a time, they went out to make phone calls to tell relatives. My mother was working desperately to get Chris on the phone, I was told. I needed so badly to hear his voice, to calm him down. I felt calm and he needed to hear that from me.

The wait felt like forever. After about five hours someone walked into the room with the phone, my mother maybe, and held it to my ear. It was Chris. He had just begun the three-hour drive to the hospital.

I wasn't crying when I spoke to him.

"I'm okay." I wanted him to know I was dealing with it. "I'm handling this, but do you know exactly what's going on? What have you been told?" I asked.

"I don't know much. Explain it to me," he said. He sounded in shock. I knew he knew what had happened, but he wanted it in my words, as though maybe my answer would be different than what he had been told, like I held the truth and it wasn't as bad as he thought.

"I'm not going to walk again. I broke my neck." I just wanted him to have the information. I didn't want to sugarcoat it for him.

He said "Okay" a couple of times but not much else. He wasn't crying either, but I could hear the shock in his voice. He didn't know how to react and suddenly became a man of few words, which was completely out of character for him. I knew he was rattled, so I just wanted to put him at ease and let him know I wasn't a mess, that I was coping. I wanted so badly for him to hear that message from me because I knew he was upset. We said good-bye and I started counting the minutes until he arrived.

It became clearer that I needed to have surgery, but we had to wait about eleven hours for some special machine to arrive. My C6 vertebra was completely shattered and the fragments had to be removed. My C5 and C7 had to be stabilized with a rod. The wait for the tools was excruciating for all of us, more so for me because I hoped Chris would get there before I went into surgery.

Oddly, my parents had gotten bad news about me once before, ironically about me walking. When I was born in Norfolk, Virginia, on October 2, 1985, the doctors weren't sure whether I would ever walk. Isn't that crazy? It was like some kind of bizarre foreshadowing. They thought I might have had spina bifida. That wasn't my only issue; I also was born with a vision impairment called nystagmus. The doctors thought even if I learned to walk, I wouldn't be able to play sports like tennis, because I wouldn't be able to see a tiny ball. I showed them on both fronts. I started playing when I was two, and I never stopped.

My parents and the doctor went out of the room at some point and told everyone in the waiting room about the surgery. A crowd of twenty-seven had gathered, apparently just for me; no other big groups were waiting for news on a loved one. All the girls from the party were still wet from the pool. The nurses brought them some blankets, and they huddled together, waiting. Some of their parents had arrived, too. The update included the information that I'd never walk again, that the damage was permanent. That was jarring news for them, as in the chaos of the accident, they had held strong to the notion that it was just a quick nerve issue that would resolve itself. This was the kind of thing that happened only to other people. That's what everyone had thought, which was why there was so much disbelief about the severity of it all. I was told everyone lost it out there—all of my girls were crying. One girl ran out, and my mom had to chase her down and hug her.

Eventually Chris arrived. He said the waiting room was absolutely quiet; he could hear people crying, but no one was talking. I had already gone into surgery, so Chris took a seat like everyone else and waited for more information. Everyone told me later that the surgery took forever. When I came out of it and people gradually came in to see me, there were tubes protruding from all over me and monitors everywhere. Most people were tall enough to sort of bend over the tubes, but my mom wasn't. They put a stool down for my mom eventually. We called it the kissing stool, because she would stand on it and could then reach in and kiss me.

I've tried to recall the first time I finally saw Chris after my surgery. There were so many drugs in my system by that point that a lot of my memories are foggy. But I do vividly remember wanting to hold his hand when I first saw him walk into my room. I was desperate for that. I couldn't ask him at the time; I couldn't speak because of the respirator down my throat. But instinctively, he did it. He reached out and grabbed my hand. I thought I'd willed him to do it. I couldn't feel him, but that didn't matter. I could feel the warmth of his hand and the pressure of it when he placed it on mine. It didn't feel the same since I couldn't hold it back, but it was comforting. I'd been craving the comfort he provides me the entire time and was so happy to have finally received it.

My bridal shower was supposed to be the next day. Needless to say, that didn't happen.

CHAPTER 6

Barely Breathing

THREE DAYS AFTER THE ACCIDENT MY HEART STOPPED, AND FOR a brief moment I was dead.

It happened, of course, in the only fifteen-minute span during which my mother left my side. From the second she arrived at the hospital, my mother, Carol, had remained awake and with me—the entire three days. She was so worried about me that she didn't want me to spend one minute alone. My blood pressure had been falling; throughout those first few days it would drop and someone would have to rush out to get the nurses.

Of course, the one time she did leave to take a small break, all hell broke loose. I was going in for what the doctors said would be a routine surgery, so she decided to take a few minutes to run home. She waited until they were wheeling me out of my room, and then she zipped out.

I don't remember anything because I'd been drugged, but basically, my heart stopped. I had to be given CPR. It was apparently extremely scary and caused major panic among the healthcare team, and it took some quick thinking to revive me. My mother was called immediately after it happened, so soon after she'd left that she hadn't even made it home. She turned right around and came back to the hospital.

My mom has always been my best friend. When I was little we had girls' nights out that my dad didn't know about. We didn't actually go out. Most nights, she'd tuck me into bed, read me a book, and rub my back while she counted to one hundred. But on some nights she would whisper "Girls' Night Out," then go to bed herself, and when my dad fell asleep, she'd sneak back into my room and grab me, and we'd put pillows and blankets down in the living room and watch Disney movies and eat popcorn late into the night. It was a really special time for me, for us both, I think. We also did so much together as I grew up. We camped and shopped and rafted and tubed. She was always a kid herself to an extent. We were a team growing up, and I knew that the aftermath of my accident was as tough on her as it was on me, maybe even more so. I was unaware then of what an enormous sacrifice she'd eventually be making for me.

I knew when I woke up in my room that my ribs seemed to really hurt and that they were bruised. I don't know how exactly, but I could feel inside of myself, like somehow my insides and my stomach could still register pressure. A day or two later, I began to wonder why my chest was still hurting. It was an odd feeling, and I noticed then that there was sort of a line between where sensation ended and where it gradually picked up again. The discomfort intensified and the pressure had increased. It began to feel like I'd been punched in the chest.

I still had a tube in my throat when a doctor came in one afternoon while I was alone, which was only because my parents and other visitors had to leave the room during a shift change for the nurses. Within that gap this doctor flat out told me my heart had stopped. I had no memory of going into cardiac arrest. There was no explanation, no comforting; he was very short and to the point about it, and then he left. I couldn't communicate or ask questions because of the tube. I was terrified. I didn't know what that meant exactly for my health or my future or anything. It was a truly awful moment. My mom and dad came in and asked me what was wrong, as my eyes were as wide as they could get. If the blow had been delivered by my family or a little more softly, perhaps I could have processed it better or easier and then moved on. Instead, that weird moment stuck with me for a while. But from then on my parents refused to leave me alone in the room even for a minute. My mom scolded the doctor later for telling me something like that without my being able to communicate.

They were supposed to put an umbrella stint into my leg to prevent blood clots. When I was in the elevator heading down for that procedure, my heart stopped.

This, of course, made me more upset. I was frustrated, mostly, that no one had told me. I didn't want to be protected like that. I wanted all of the information I could get my hands on. Information was helping me cope and process the situation. I had been strong up until then, so I didn't want anyone to think I was too fragile to know or hear about what was happening to me and what exactly I was dealing with. Information, as hard as it was to hear, was reassuring. Being informed was comforting.

After that some days went well and some days were really terrifying. Everyone would describe it as a roller coaster. There were random things happening all the time to my body while I was in the hospital. My lung collapsed while I was in the ICU, for example. I didn't have the ability to cough and I wasn't moving around, so mucous and congestion entered into my system and had the potential to cause pneumonia. The stickiness of the mucous essentially made the two sides of my lung walls stick together, and when that occurs no air can go in. I couldn't breathe. I remember one day that suddenly I couldn't get enough air, and I felt panicked.

The resolution to that problem, which happened often, was pretty horrific, too. The nurses would suck the mucous out with a tube that had suction. On days when it became really bad, they'd put the tube up my nose and down my nasal passage, into my throat, while I was completely awake, and it would suck all the mucous out from my lungs while I was sitting up. It was the most horrible feeling ever, but at the end of it I knew I would be able to breathe. They had a screen that showed what was going on in my lungs, and they could see exactly how much congestion had built up. If there was more and they needed to go in, I'd say, "Just do it again, just go for it and get it over with." The mucous made me feel like I was going to puke and gag, so the procedure became the easy part. The doctors told me no one had ever asked for them to go back in. I realized then I was pretty brave.

One of the most traumatizing experiences of my entire injury was in the ICU. When the tube that cleared my lungs wasn't doing it well enough, the doctors had to perform an even more intricate procedure. Once, before the procedure began, I was lying on my side and they were missing a part to this machine that they were assembling. I was sitting there with one lung, barely able to breathe, and I didn't want to freak out, because it would only make me breathe harder. But it was so hard to be calm, watching these people put together the machine. Then, as soon as they figured it out, there was no warning, just, "Let's do this." It happened so fast. I went from nothing—from sitting and watching them for what felt like forever—to being drugged (but not drugged correctly) to undergoing a traumatic procedure. I was trying not to overanalyze anything because I was trying not to scare myself. I *was* scared, but I was literally talking to myself in my head, saying, *Chill out. This is a procedure that I want to have, and everything will feel so much better when it is over.*

Ideally, if the procedure goes according to plan, the doctors put you half asleep, not in full anesthesia, but they give you just enough drugs to knock you out. Then they take a big scope, which is much bigger than you'd think, and put it down your throat to suck the mucous out. This time when they started the procedure, they didn't give me enough drugs, maybe because of the rush to get started after the delay in assembling the machine. But I was too awake. I began to freak out, so they gave me more drugs, and it knocked me into this weird semisleep; I was kind of awake and not awake at the same time. All the drugs were making me hallucinate, so I remember that—this was scary and traumatizing—I had a dream in which there was a barbaric war and people were putting a sword down my throat. I vividly remember the pain. This was the worst thing I ever felt, because it was not only physically but also mentally scary. It was the weirdest thing, being drugged up but awake enough to know that what was happening to me was bad. When I fully woke up, I don't think anyone was aware of what I had just endured.

After the surgery they threw me on a hard metal plate in order to take an X-ray of my chest to see what they had accomplished, and because my body had experienced a lot of physical trauma just days before, lying on a hard surface was extremely painful. So I awoke from this horrible dream only to be thrown onto a metal table, and I felt like no one was listening to me, but I could barely speak. It was a bad experience. I was trying to tell them how much pain I was in, but it was just a lot of chaos and noise; there were too many people, and I couldn't explain what had happened. The nostril suction was almost a daily occurrence initially. The sword procedure happened twice, and only the second time was it a horror show. But I never cried.

CHAPTER 7

One Day at a Time

SOMEONE MADE A BOARD FOR ME ON A GIANT ORANGE PIECE OF poster paper, writing the entire alphabet on it so I could spell out what I wanted to say, letter by letter. Visitors would touch a letter with their finger and I would nod when they got it correct. It took a little time getting used to communicating like this, which was rough, but once we had a system in place for pointing to letters, I could at least be understood. The first name I spelled out was that of the friend I knew would be having the hardest time with the accident. I wanted to know if she was okay. I would point out one name at a time, but almost daily, I returned to asking about her. No one had really asked me about who pushed me, even though the families all knew. No one outside of the core group was told. It was one topic that was left alone, maybe out of respect for us both. Everyone just knew not to talk about it.

I was able to communicate through this board that I wasn't angry. And I wasn't. Not at my friend or any of the girls there that night, not at myself, and not at what had happened. I didn't cry and I wasn't angry. We had a lot of laughs along the way as I tried to communicate all of this, but I was able to at least acknowledge how I was feeling, try to console everyone who was upset, and thank them for being there for me. I told them I was there for them, too. I wanted them to be okay. Even later when I could talk, I informed them over and over again, "I am totally fine." I think they suspected I was more hurt than I was portraying, which is half true, half not true, but they were just trying to protect me. I was processing information pretty darn well in spite of everything.

After the whirlwind at the very beginning, where there was an urgency to my treatment, after everyone caught their breath and the initial shock began to subside, deeper conversations with the girls really began. Step one was obviously getting myself stabilized and knowing the physical challenges that were ahead of me. That was the most important element of recovery. Next, of course, was the mental aspect of it. Everyone by the pool had had some time to really process, at least to a certain extent, exactly what had happened.

We had a couple of group discussions. The girls wanted to be certain there was no anger. Once I could speak, I was clearer about this: I wasn't holding back. I wasn't angry at all. I think because I hadn't really shown a lot of emotion, they thought I was repressing my feelings. Even at this point, when I was getting stronger, they were still crying. I'd heard they cried together in the ICU. They were extremely upset and traumatized. I had to help them, and this was the first time I realized it was up to me to be the spine for the group. Even though they were still quite emotional, they were there for me, really there. They visited a lot, they talked, they helped, and they were committed. It was a nice feeling to experience that kind of love from friends.

One of the girls told me she'd initially been worried that Chris might leave me, but after seeing us together, and witnessing how he had responded and cared for me, she wasn't worried anymore. She saw our love firsthand and realized we were both strong individually and our love was strong, too.

I don't think anyone doubted my strength beforehand, but it was never really put to the test until this accident, so it was never questioned. I never had anyone ask me to think about what would happen if my life took this kind of turn. Who thinks of those things? In this case, there was nothing that had happened to even compare it to. It was a bizarre situation. I couldn't say how anyone else would handle it. Every day was one day at a time.

Whenever I felt my mind going into a negative place, I literally told myself to stop. I didn't want negative thoughts to send me spiraling downward into a depression or rage. I never allowed it to get to that point, and it wasn't just for all of my friends and family; it was for me, too. It was simply a fight-or-flight response for me, a coping mechanism, as if my brain told me not to cry because crying would be bad. Crying wouldn't do me any good. I didn't want to feel like crying or being close to tears, and so I would tell a joke or request that my friends come in and then talk to them constantly. I was never alone with my thoughts.

Looking back, sure, that might have been avoidance. Maybe. But at the time it still got me through it.

～～

The tears eventually fell, but not exactly because of my situation as a whole. I cried about incidents that occurred but not where life had taken me. One time, I thought my fingers moved. I was always trying to move them, and I could have sworn that one finally did, and I remember telling my dad that it was the one thing that I wanted back. I had been in a hospital bed in the ICU for six days, and my dad was in the room. I moved my wrist, and it appeared as if my finger had moved. I said, "Dad, my finger moved!" I cried out of happiness then. If my wrist moved even slightly, it made it look like my finger moved. I saw what looked like a twitch for the very first time, and I gasped quietly with happiness because I thought movement and function were returning in my fingers.

Having movement in my fingers would have meant a lot, because small twitches like that are significant. From what I'd heard it would have been a good indication that I'd recover finger movement someday. I'd heard that if you started feeling your digits five or six days after breaking your neck, that was good. In the big picture it would have meant touch, and an ability to do my own hair, or to hold Chris's hand back when he held mine, or a million other small things we take for granted each day.

It's funny how even then everyone was saying, "She can't walk." Walk, walk, walk, walk. I wasn't even thinking about my legs. In the beginning I didn't even know what was moving and what was not. But by the sixth or the seventh day, I was trying to pick up things and use my hands, and I realized, *All I want is my hands back.* I began to understand how much regaining finger function would mean to my life and how drastic an impact it had on my day-to-day functioning. It was one of those things I hadn't given any thought to before: my fingers and the importance they play in my life. Suddenly, they'd become almost everything, monumental.

A woman from physical therapy came in for an evaluation, and she held my hand to see if I had any twitches or flickers of the muscle. She felt something, too, and it reinforced the idea that I had in fact made my finger move. I got really excited, but I think I knew deep down that my fingers weren't exactly working.

Sadly, she was wrong and I was right. I waited for my fingers to work again, desperately searching for a sign they would, but eventually I realized they weren't doing anything at all. There were no more twitches. There really hadn't ever been any. I learned about my wrist and how it was making my fingers appear to move. I was slowly relearning my body and realizing that there were muscles I hadn't even thought about that weren't receiving the signal from my brain to move. It wasn't one heartbreaking moment or day. I just eventually realized over time that my fingers weren't going to move.

It's a toss-up between feeling sex and moving my fingers, but I think fingers would be all I would ask to have back if I could, more than anything else.

CHAPTER 8

Support from Friends

As soon as I regained my voice a few days into my hospital stay, I was cracking jokes. There was one extremely happy and hilarious moment when Samantha brought my first McDonald's meal during my stay—it was such a treat. It's funny that having that burger and fries is one of my greatest memories, but it thrilled me to no end and I was grateful she had smuggled it in. It's so memorable because we laughed pretty hard about how excited I was about fast food.

There were a lot of little laughs, mostly because I didn't want to live in a somber, stressful environment. I know my upbeat attitude and ability to laugh off a lot of things was a concern for some people, because they thought I was burying my pain. But when I said I wasn't hiding anything, I wasn't. It wasn't as if I sat there thinking, *I'm not going to share my feelings with anyone.* I truly wasn't able to cry and I was finding humor in my day-to-day, even in the hospital. Crying is what people expect, I guess—the reaction that reveals to others what's in your head. Maybe I didn't process it all, but I didn't have the ability to cry or scream out; that hadn't come to me yet in those early hospital days. I just didn't have the urge to do that. I was obviously scared and sad, but when you're in that kind of situation, you're simply not thinking about five or six months down the road; you're in the hospital and you're just sick. I was in that moment, trying to get through that day. I wasn't thinking about not being able to walk; I was just trying to cope with the challenges of that particular day.

I was told that there were never fewer than fifteen people in the waiting room at any given time. The girls fastened together little pieces of purple and gold ribbon and handed them out to my visitors to pin onto themselves and wear as they arrived. My grandparents came with doughnuts every morning, and on some days other people brought food, too. I couldn't join in, but the Monday after my accident, everyone tailgated out in back of the hospital, consuming all the food they'd had ready for my bridal shower. They got in trouble from security for lighting up a barbecue grill in the parking lot. It was nice, having all these friends. Everyone popped into my room that day and read notes to me, and the support made me feel really good.

Although it was lovely to have so many people around me and to notice improvement daily, I had grown increasingly aware that there would be no wedding anytime soon. I knew, of course, there would be one eventually, but not for a long time.

People slowly started spreading the word that our big day was postponed until further notice. Each relative took the time to contact the people they knew who were invited to let them know what was happening and advise them to cancel their travel plans. On CaringBridge.com, my mom and Samantha posted updates on my recovery and said that the wedding was on hold. My paternal grandmother, Bubbie, and grandfather, Zadie, were paying for the wedding originally, so she ended up cancelling a lot of the food orders and other arrangements. While many brides might have sobbed at the thought of their wedding being postponed, I was just so focused on getting through my injuries and figuring out where my life was going to end up that the wedding wasn't even a blip. I was excited about it, but I knew it would happen anyway someday. I focused more on healing and rehabbing.

Understandably, all of the energy and concern was directed toward me. Chris, my parents and relatives, everyone put their vibes toward my healing, sometimes at the expense of their own. No one put his or her own health aside more than my mother. Her friend Margie had fortunately come to town to provide my mom with some needed support. One night at midnight the two of them dashed out to get some items they needed at Kmart (and probably Margie wanted to give her a break from the hospital), and they jumped on the carousel there as a release. She said they barely fit, but it was nice to laugh and enjoy a bit of a distraction during an intense time.

Despite tiny reprieves like that, the stress of constantly being on-call for me took its toll. One day, toward the end of my stay in the ICU, my mom left to take a quick shower in Margie's hotel near the hospital. Out of nowhere, half of my mom's left eye went dark. She said later she thought it was because her own blood pressure had increased (she'd been monitoring mine). But it wasn't; it was because of exhaustion, and she wound up being admitted to the hospital for three days herself. She was in a wheelchair, but at the time I had no idea. She'd get wheeled to my room from her room, which I didn't even know existed, and she'd stand up outside and then come into my room as if nothing had happened. She would leave at a certain time to return to her room, and although I never asked why I knew she didn't want me to see her sick like that. She didn't want anyone to worry about her, not me and not friends who had been coming and going during my stay in the ICU.

At around the ten-day mark, my dad asked the doctors often how long I'd be in the hospital. We never were given a solid idea of just how long it would be, and my parents and Chris began discussing rehab and trying to figure out where I'd go next. They were trying to develop a plan for that. The woman at the hospital who handled the rehab process came rushing in one day when only my mother was there with me and said a spot had opened up at a facility in Greenville. She said if we didn't take that spot, it would be given to someone else. We literally had thirty minutes to figure this all out, and my mother was the only one available to decide. It was incredibly stressful for her, and we were frustrated that we had gotten so few answers on all the days we had asked, then all of a sudden it was, "Take this, or who knows." We took the spot in Greenville, unsure if we were making the right decision. The next day, I was whisked off.

CHAPTER 9

Rockin' Rehab

My girls really made my room in rehab rock. It became a cool place to hang out. They hung up a small whiteboard to replace the alphabet board from the hospital, and they decorated the room to make it fun as well. The white message board became the focal point of my friends' and my recovery. I didn't need it to communicate because I could talk by this point, but the board symbolized a lot. People wrote some fun and crazy messages on it. One of the girls drew a palm tree and a beach scene for me, so I could be at my favorite place. "Go Pirates" was also a regular message. People wrote words of love and inspiration and even jokes on this whiteboard. It was a place for everyone to share his or her feelings. Of course, "Let It Be" was a daily mantra. It was written up there and never erased.

The original alphabet board survived the hospital and became part of the rehab decor. One of the girls wrote "You a Badass" at the bottom of the letter board they'd created in the hospital and hung it up as well. She remembered me saying I was badass when the ambulance workers arrived. They even hung an ECU Pirates flag over my bed, and the football and basketball coaches sent me autographed balls. I had an ECU throw, too. Lauren's sister-in-law was a Redskins cheerleader, so she arranged for an autographed squad photo to be sent my way. The girls made it so much fun and so lively in a place that usually isn't colorful in any way. This was such a troubling circumstance to be in, but we still all managed to laugh and have a good time with the cards that had been dealt.

The matter of who had pushed me hadn't really surfaced up to this point. We all felt concern for that friend, and we kept the dialogue very open about the status of my health and how everyone was feeling. But at this point in my recovery, no really serious issues had emerged from that girl. She seemed, on the surface, to be dealing with any guilt constructively, showing up like everyone else. I thought she had gotten through it okay. Maybe in my heart I worried just a little that it would all boil up at some point, but I wasn't sure.

Despite the gravity of my situation, we tried to have fun and find peace in rehab. It was actually a really fun time, as odd as that might sound. Some of the laughs we had there were the best laughs we'd ever had.

Sometimes, we'd have so much fun that we'd get into trouble. A couple of us figured out where they kept the power wheelchairs. I would get into one, and one or two of my friends would get into one, and we'd go to this really big hallway at the main hospital section of where I was in rehab. It was really straight, and it went on forever. Each chair had two buttons for speed. One had a picture of a rabbit, obviously for fast, and one had a picture of a turtle, for slower movement. I thought that was hilarious. So we'd get in the chairs, and we'd race up and down the hallway. I'd win the most, as I recall. Once we were really moving and this grumpy front desk woman came out and started yelling at us to stop. We stopped briefly, but once she left, we went right back at it. What were they going to do, kick me out?

We participated in calmer activities that made me equally happy. I had grown up singing and was afraid I'd never be able to sing again without a strong diaphragm and core muscles. I hadn't lost my voice, but I couldn't yell or scream or even speak very loudly. It was twenty times harder to find the strength to sing, but while I was in the rehab I did sing again; I worked hard to get to that point. One day, Carly and I went into the all-purpose room where they had a piano, and we began to sing as we often did before my injury. I wasn't thinking about my injury but about how happy singing made me feel. It became something we did together during rehab. People would stop in the halls and listen to us. Our bond was strong, as it was with all of my friends from that night. It always had been, but it was more so following the accident.

Samantha, Lauren, Britney, and Carly had different schedules and lived in different cities, so they coordinated their visits so that at least one of them came to rehab most days. Carly was around a lot, maybe the most after the accident. All four of them were there, but she had a flexible work schedule that allowed her to visit more often. She even slept there sometimes. Now, when something like this happens, you get pretty used to things you might otherwise be bothered by. Carly did two really big things for me that showed me how much she loved me.

Since I couldn't use my fingers and my nose was full of, well, junk, I was often uncomfortable. Carly went the extra mile and early on would actually pick my nose. I mean, Chris had to do that, too, and I love him for it, but a girlfriend? It was unbelievable what a good sport she was about that.

Also, I got used to people seeing me naked. Carly was with me in the hospital one day when a nurse was inserting a catheter into me. The nurse was explaining to my mom how it would have to be done and when. I was concerned because in addition to everything else, my mom and Chris were going to have to deal with this after I left rehab. There were just so many things they were going to have to do for me because of my lack of dexterity. Carly jumped right in.

"Would it be helpful if I learned how to do that?" she asked my mom.

"Sure," she said. "It would be a big help whenever you come to visit."

I laughed. "Carly, would you really do that? You're prepared to get all up in my business down there to help?"

"Sure. We're close, aren't we?" she asked.

The nurse began explaining right then and there. Carly learned to insert a catheter into my urethra, so I could go to the bathroom. I think the nurse was even moved. That's friendship. That's love. I think we women, as a group, underestimate our power. Our collective power. I think we all know the power of love between a couple. That's completely different and significant. But the power of friendship and love between female friends? It's amazing, and it was something as simple as a catheter insertion that had a profound impact on me and my realization of this power we can all harness by sticking together.

CHAPTER 10

The Proposal

CHRIS'S PROPOSAL HAPPENED WHEN I WAS LEAST EXPECTING IT. It was July 11, 2009. It took a minute or less, which is funny, since I had spent my entire life waiting for that minute.

Before it happened, things were really shaping up in our lives. I had finally landed an amazing job working for the parks and recreation department part time that summer, and we'd bought our first home together. We had adopted a sweet yellow Lab, and Chris had finished his first year of teaching. It felt like it was really the perfect time to take that next step with one another, and I was ready for a ring. Really ready. I patiently waited, day after day, expecting on every occasion he would pull out a ring. I was reading into his every thought and movement all summer to try to guess when it would happen. On our four-year anniversary, we went to the 65th Street spot, *our street,* where we had first started dating. It was so romantic. We talked for hours on the beach, then made love under the stars, and it was amazing. At the end of the night, I was basically shocked that Chris hadn't pulled out a ring. It was a setup made for a marriage proposal. Like a Hollywood movie setup. Yet he didn't ask me.

Then on the Fourth of July we took his parents' boat out on the lake to watch the local fireworks. As we cuddled at the front of the boat, he grabbed me and kissed me softly. I couldn't even focus, because my thoughts were so preoccupied with this possible proposal. The fireworks ended, and we began to head back to the house. Another opportunity lost. I realized I needed to stop being such a girl and just let it happen. So I put my proposal obsession aside and went about my summer. I think he wanted to catch me off guard, and he really did.

We were at a fancy restaurant one night called Freemason Abbey, and after we finished our drinks, he got out of his seat. At first I barely noticed what was happening. He stood up abruptly without saying anything, and I was thinking, *Where is he going?* Then he got down on one knee.

"Will you be my wife?" he asked.

I exclaimed, "Yes!" I was startled. I think I said it ten times over and over again.

He pulled out a ring and said, "This is my grandmother's ring. I will buy you your own when we can afford it."

It was a princess-cut diamond in a yellow gold setting, and it was beautiful. He'd spoken to his mom and told her that he couldn't afford a ring but that he wanted to propose. She had some family jewels, so they sorted through them and chose this one. He stood up and announced to the restaurant, "This is Rachelle, and she just agreed to be my wife!" Everyone clapped. Then we kissed.

Then Chris started to lead me upstairs right away. The restaurant had enormously high ceilings, flanked with wood paneling and a huge rustic chandelier hanging low. It had this zigzag staircase that led up to the balcony seating. I was so confused as to why we were on the move like this, leaving our table, but I was so giddy, filled with joy, surprised, and excited, that I didn't ask any questions. I looked up and I realized both of our entire families were there! I hadn't even seen them, but they had watched the entire proposal, and we were all able to have dinner and celebrate together. Some were waiting on the stairs, and we all hugged. It was such a perfect night. He took my breath away.

—◦—

Sadly, many people asked if Chris and I would still be together after the accident, but even in the hospital that doubt never crossed our minds. We were deeply in love, and the accident didn't change that. In fact, I felt sorry for the people who asked because it suggested to me that they didn't know true love. It was essentially the most asked question. It was crazy. Honestly, if given the opportunity to walk again, but having to do so without him, I wouldn't do it. Our love proved to be far more powerful than this accident.

I believed in love and soul mates, and I knew through Chris that dreams came true. But I didn't believe everything happened for a reason. I didn't believe that if I simply worked hard, I'd walk again. I hated when people said things like that. It implied that everyone in a chair wasn't trying hard enough. That they just didn't want it bad enough. People also said that I was so positive that surely I would walk again. Positivity doesn't make you stand up. It's like telling an amputee that if he's positive and tries hard enough, his leg will grow back. My spinal cord was an actual thing that broke, soft like a banana, easy to snap. I didn't have a disease I was fighting through. I had damaged my spinal cord. If you unplug a lamp, no matter how hard you try, or how positive you are, it will not turn on. I believed in science, and since I was still young, maybe when I was fifty someone would develop something that would allow me to walk again one day—even if it was only for twenty or thirty years of my life.

All along I knew Chris and I were supposed to be together, not meant to be. That was the only place I got confused about pre-destiny a bit, when I pondered why all of this happened, knowing there was no good answer. Chris and I were *supposed to be* because we were the right fit for each other, the perfect match, but I'm not sure if we were *predestined,* though the differentiation confused me when I thought about it. I didn't believe I was *meant to be* injured, or predestined to spend my life unable to walk. That's why it confused me a bit when it came to our love; it was the only thing that I couldn't square because otherwise our relationship was so perfect, it felt like we were soul mates. I felt like I'd die without him; I couldn't breathe were he not there. I realized it was hypocritical to say you believe in soul mates but you don't believe in fate. It's kind of convenient: Some good things are meant to be and bad things are not, and maybe fate steps in sometimes. There is a passage in the Zohar, a set of books on Jewish mysticism, that says that one soul comes down to earth but it's split into two. One part goes to a baby boy and the other part to a baby girl, and if they be worthy, God reunites them in marriage. So you have to be a good person to get that other part of your soul. You won't necessarily be together for sure, but your choices make you worthy of finding your soul mate or not. Maybe that's the case. Maybe it's not.

It was a dilemma I struggled with often beyond the question about love. Many people e-mailed me and commented on news stories about my accident, saying that it was "God's will" and "Everything happened for a reason." There are so many awful things that occur in our world, and I found it difficult to believe that any higher power would purposely cause people pain. I just refused to believe that. A horrific event like Sandy Hook couldn't have been God's will. Kidnapping of children can't be God's will. Terrible diseases can't be God's will. My never walking can't be God's will. I like to believe if there is a higher power, he or she wouldn't do such terrible things to people.

I was raised Jewish, and I went to Hebrew school twice a week and Sunday school once a week, but in my household I was simply raised with morals and taught to be a nice person. At times religious people said, "Be good, so you can go to heaven" or "Because that's what God wants," but I didn't want to be good to go to heaven; I wanted to be good because it was the right thing to do. So religion wasn't a big thing for me, though I knew it had helped a lot of people and I didn't begrudge anyone who clung to it. I didn't pray or talk to any higher power or base my decision on any religion or higher power. I just went about my life as a moral person.

Honestly, more than a church, Chris and I had a place on the beach that was our place to reflect, and it was meaningful for us. It was the 65th Street spot. That night we started our relationship, we didn't kiss, but the next day we went on a date to a restaurant called the Duck Inn. The restaurant was a Virginia Beach staple. I had had my prom there and lifeguard banquets there. It was just one of those places with a lot of history. We ate seafood, and when the bill came he paid, a courtesy I wasn't used to at all. After dinner we went to our spot on the beach, the one where we had just stayed up all night talking. We put down a blanket, and I remember him leaning into me, and we kissed with the sound of waves crashing, the smell of the ocean making me so happy.

In rehab I looked back on those days, and I was so proud that I knew how good I had it. I believed, even then, that we, as humans, have the power to make something positive of a bad situation. While I don't believe that "everything happens for a reason," I believe we can give anything a purpose, even a negative situation. Good things came from my injury because I made the decision for that to happen, not because it was predestined to happen.

With Chris, I just felt like I had to have him, every moment. If we weren't together, I wouldn't be the same person. If that was taken away from me, I wouldn't be able to breathe. I felt that a soul mate was a person who made you the best that you could be, made you happy, made you want to live life and wake up.

During my time in the hospital and rehab, everyone marveled at how Chris knew, almost instinctively, how to make me comfortable. He knew me so well. My dad said later he was impressed by how quickly Chris fell into that routine as the person to defer to, and even the doctors turned to him to ask questions. He was my other half for better or worse. He knew.

CHAPTER 11

The Big Day, Take One

INSTEAD OF SPENDING JUNE GETTING READY TO MARRY CHRIS, I'd spent it trying to survive and then learning about how life would be at rehab. I had sat in a wheelchair for the first time on June 5 instead of organizing who was sitting where at the wedding. I was learning how to feed myself and how to use the remaining strength in my arms to push my wheelchair instead of making last-minute floral arrangements or talking to the DJ about the music.

Since the accident Chris and my mom had gotten into a pattern of switching off, making sure each night one person stayed with me. There was a tiny chair that pulled out into a poor excuse for a bed. One night Chris and I were lying there in the dark, and we were talking. We both were aware our wedding date was approaching, just days away.

We should have been sleeping or trying to fall asleep, but Chris was talking through some feelings of guilt I hadn't realized he had.

"I hate seeing you like this," he said. "I was supposed to protect you, and I wasn't there to do it."

I didn't say anything. My heart broke for him. I knew he was suffering badly and it was bubbling up to the surface at that moment.

Then he broke down and said, "I just wish I had danced with you more. I'm really sorry, because now we can't."

All I could say was, "It's okay, sweetie."

He doesn't cry often. We just cried together and hugged that night. There was nothing that could be said. I could see the sadness in him that night, and I didn't want that for him. I didn't want him to feel regret or any kind of guilt at all. But it was the saddest moment of my stay. At that moment I wanted out. I didn't want to be in rehab anymore. I didn't want to be in this situation. I wanted to be dancing at my wedding. His tears were too much for me to hold it together.

—~—

June 27, 2010, arrived, the day that would have been my wedding. I didn't wake up with butterflies in my stomach and anticipation like I should have, and while I was disappointed, I wasn't sad. I knew we'd get there, but I had to get well first. It was hard to imagine during those days how different my June had become.

Still, we had a huge party at the rehab facility to mark the day. We'd briefly discussed getting married right then and there in the garden at the facility, but I was concerned that would mean the accident would have taken the dream wedding idea away from me. I wanted the real deal regardless, so ultimately we decided to wait.

I obviously couldn't get dolled up clothing-wise that day, but everyone was casual for our little celebration. It was a jeans and T-shirt party for sure. Samantha was excellent at hair and makeup; on most visits she'd fix me up. So on this day, my would-be wedding, she styled my hair and applied my makeup in my room before everyone arrived.

As we got ready that day, she said, "You look so pretty."

"Thanks," I said, "even in my bum clothes!"

"Yes. And you'll look even prettier on your actual wedding day. We're all holding on for that and can't wait."

"I'm excited about that day happening," I said.

"We all are, too," Samantha said.

My aunt and uncle, my parents, Chris, all the rest of the girls, and Chris's family were there—everyone brought great food, and we took over the multipurpose room to celebrate. My mom brought Funfetti cupcakes, which are my absolute favorite. There was watermelon, too. There's a really great place in Greenville called Parker's BBQ and someone brought food from there, which was a nice break from the food I'd been eating for the past four weeks. It was like we had a big backyard BBQ celebration, but in this little rehab room with Wi-Fi and a big-screen TV instead of at someone's house. It was just as fun.

At some point while we were eating, we heard some commotion coming from the hallway. We all quieted our chatting to have a listen, and all of a sudden some senior citizens that I had taught cheerleading to came busting into the room. I had taken them on when I was the activities coordinator at their center. They represented our town at the Senior Games. They were in uniform and everything, cheering "L-E-T-S G-O, let's go, let's go, L-E-T-S G-O! Gooooo RACHELLE!" As I sat there watching, I realized that these women, even though they were forty years older than me, were my friends. My heart warmed at the thought.

Everyone clapped, and I was completely moved. It was so nice of them to do this. The entire thing was a true celebration with lots of laughs, and not a tear was shed. We were all happy to be together, all my closest family and friends. Chris and I stayed together that night. We spent the night holding each other and talking about our future plans and how much we loved each other. I will say, in the morning when I woke up, I felt a little sad. I should have been on my honeymoon trip to the Bahamas. I should have been running up and down on the beach in a bikini with my new husband. I should have been married. That was when reality hit me.

CHAPTER 12

Finding Peace

ABOUT A MONTH INTO REHAB, AROUND THE END OF JUNE, I TOOK my first trip out of the hospital. We went to a park I used to go to for fun and concerts. It felt nice to be outside while I was still recovering. I was turning a corner mentally and physically, and I was aware of that.

My parents, Chris, and my friend Rebecca came along, and they wheeled me to the park. We sat there and enjoyed a concert. I hadn't been outside since my injury, so I was taking it all in. I felt a little nostalgic and maybe a little bit sad. It was my first time back in that park in a while, and I couldn't help but look around and think back to when I had *walked* around the grounds. It was situated next to the river my mom and I had gone kayaking on when she came to visit me when I was in college there. Rehab and my college were in the same town, so I was surrounded by history. Walking history. Able-bodied history. I tried to explain how I was feeling to everyone.

"It's so weird to be here, because I have so many good memories from this place," I said.

My dad said, "Well, now you'll make new memories."

It was a simple yet profound statement.

He said, "It's actually a really good and important philosophy to make new memories every single day, especially now that you are healing. We shouldn't live for old ones. We should live for new ones."

Those were some smart and powerful words, and I decided to make a daily effort during my recovery to live by them. It became my approach to all of this change. Later, my friend Rebecca, after pondering what my dad had said, wrote me an e-mail saying that she'd thought a lot about the statement and that it was true—there was so much more ahead of me. It was really nice to hear from her, knowing she'd given it as much thought as I had. That she was as moved by this simple concept: Life goes on and we make new memories every day, regardless of our situation or the hand we've been dealt. The note she sent made me realize something else, too: that my life and this accident had an impact on everyone around me.

Arriving at the understanding that all would be okay happened there in rehab, but it was a gradual process. It didn't mean I was okay with my injury—obviously, given the chance to change it, of course I would have. But the reality was that I couldn't, so I found peace instead of beating myself up over my situation. It wasn't about complacency; it was about dealing with what I had to deal with and knowing that making peace helped.

I can't pinpoint the exact moment it occurred, but in rehab I just realized, "It is what it is." I said that to myself a lot. I had to manage myself because no one was going to do that for me. I had to *let it be*. There was never a time when I was angry, but there were definitely spurts of sadness. I would always make jokes with the therapist, and then I would break down a little bit at night, when it was quiet and I was alone and wasn't being kept busy.

And that was natural to me. Of course I'd break down. Of course I was sad, but overall I realized there was nothing I could do to change what had happened. I couldn't go backward; I couldn't stay where I was, so I had to move forward. I simply didn't want to be a depressed, negative person; I wanted to be myself. So I went forward with the same personality that I'd always had for the sake of my own mental health and for the sake of Chris. It wouldn't have been fair for him to not only part with me physically but also lose me as a person. I knew my physical condition would not be the end of us and that he deserved to have the woman he set out to marry originally.

Another woman, Frances, really defined friendship for me. She was in rehab and helped me through a lot of tough moments. She was a volunteer and a quadriplegic herself, and she would visit me often. I had a lot in common with her. She was hurt in her twenties like me and was also very active. We had both taught aerobics. We had similar functions. She gave me some pointers on how to apply makeup. I learned through Frances that I was able to do a lot with my arms. I realized that there was no horizontal line cutting off my feeling and function, but that my biceps, wrists, and shoulders had a lot of strength and could compensate for my lack of triceps, so with time, I would gain mobility. For example, when applying foundation, I learned to pour it onto the palm of my hand and wipe it on my face. I had enough strength to lift my arms to do that. With eyeliner, I squeezed the stick together with two hands and could apply it.

Frances explained to me that I could ultimately do a lot with the strength in my wrist, like feed myself and eventually drive. She had a caregiver who helped her in the mornings and evenings, but Frances did many things on her own. She cleaned her own pool at home, washed her own car, and gardened. It was so motivating and enlightening. She kept me positive in general and was someone to laugh with and even ask the personal questions that no medical professionals could really answer.

Frances had a huge part in my recovery. I wouldn't have been as positive without her as my mentor and my friend. She was there every single day, and we spoke for hours. I asked her hundreds and hundreds of questions over the two and a half months I was there.

Laughter helped, too. Samantha had a little Chihuahua named Marley. I don't usually like that kind of dog, but I was really missing my Lab. One day, she showed up and opened her purse.

I said, "Oh my God, you brought your dog!"

She said, "Yeah, why not? No one will care."

I explained we had to keep it on the down-low.

She had smuggled little Marley into rehab, past everyone who might have tossed her and the doggie out. All to cheer me up. You can't have animals in hospitals unless they're certified therapy dogs, so this was really breaking the rules.

We had to involve the nurse on duty because she was in the room a lot. But we knew she wouldn't tell on us. We also needed to keep the door closed and instituted a password for entry. I'm not sure why, but I decided the code word was "chicken leg." So family and the nurse would be coming in and out, and that day they had to say "chicken leg" every single time they knocked. Sam and I laughed so hard that we cried. It was one fun afternoon for sure.

CHAPTER 13

Love and Sex

PART OF REHAB WAS GETTING USED TO REAL LIFE AFTER THE hospital. And for me, that meant sex. So one day in late July during rehab, Chris and I were given the opportunity to stay together in a room within the hospital that was set up like a small apartment. The idea was that we were on our own that night to practice what it would be like when I went home. The nurses were a phone call away, just in case. Frances had given me a lot of information on how sex was going to be following the accident, and it was helpful for me to have my expectations in order.

We were finally alone for the first time in two months in this tiny room that looked like a nice hotel room, complete with floral comforter and small TV. I was simply happy to lie beside him, wrapped up in his arms. I can't describe how painful it was to have to endure months without being able to lie in bed cuddling and embracing the one you love, but instead having to be in a hospital bed alone. We hadn't been intimate in months, and we were previously an extremely sexual couple. I longed to share that with him again, but I knew it would be different. I could no longer feel below my chest, so I wasn't sure this was even going to be enjoyable. But I quickly realized that it wasn't about having an orgasm.

It was about being with him. Before, sex was all about the final result, and now it was more intimate, more personal, passionate, and loving. This time, we didn't totally know what we were doing. It was a lot like losing my virginity again.

It was my first time sleeping in a real bed since the accident. I still wore a neck brace, which wasn't very sexy, but we worked with it. I was no longer able to move all around, but I laid flat on my back and I was able to wrap my arms around him. I was told that the parts of your body that you can feel, particularly your neck, become more sensitive, and it was true. I learned where I was sensitive and where I hadn't acknowledged being sensitive before. That night was incredibly intense, more intense than the physical sex we'd had before the accident. This time it was emotional; it was making love. It certainly wasn't better than the physical relationship we'd shared, which I was sad to have lost, but at least I knew there was hope and that we would still be able to find a way to remain physically connected.

Chris was my first and only. We dated for a few months, and in October 2005 I lost my virginity to him. It was an emotional experience for me, because I had waited a long time to find the right person. It was my sophomore year of college, about a week after my twentieth birthday, and it was one of those things that was perfectly set up. By now I had moved into a house with two of my friends and they weren't going to be there; it was our only opportunity to be by ourselves, so it had to be that night. We both knew it was going to happen, so I was very nervous. I was thinking, *I am not going to be a virgin anymore.* How many twenty-year-olds do you know who are virgins? The poor guy had a lot of pressure on him. But I had no expectations at the time—I just wanted to be with the man I had fallen in love with.

I felt at that moment in time that Chris really was the one. With the lights out we made love and he told me he loved me. It was beautiful. It was great, being with him and knowing he'd be the only man I'd ever sleep with. I didn't cry, but I got misty-eyed sharing that moment with him.

The first time Chris told me he loved me was two weeks after we'd started dating. We had made out on my grandma's couch. He whispered something in my ear. I wasn't sure if I'd heard correctly, that he'd said, "I love you," so I couldn't say it back. But then I sat up and looked at him and asked, "Did you just say 'I love you'?" He nodded. I said, "I love you, too."

My mother and father weren't strict with me at all, but there was always a mutual respect and an open line of communication. My mother always said, "Don't have sex until you find someone who is worth it. Wait until you meet someone you care for and who cares for you." I listened to that. I believed she was sharing the best advice with me, and I was glad I listened. I had waited until I found someone who loved me, and I wouldn't have wanted it any other way.

Obviously sex had become different for me after the accident, and it was also one of the things that I had taken for granted. We were a sexual couple before the accident; we connected deeply in that sense, and to have an orgasm taken away from me was incredibly hard, but we compensated. It just wasn't natural to not be able to do that. Honestly, I still enjoyed sex and I still got excited. Even though I couldn't feel sex, my brain still received signals of pleasure. I got a tingling feeling all over, but it wasn't like a peak and a finish. It was not an orgasm, followed by the type of release an able-bodied person might feel. But at times I felt my body and mind were more relaxed when we'd finished.

Rehab at the hospital was a really important element to my recovery—sex was only one aspect of that recovery. There were so many layers to getting better. I knew I wouldn't walk, but that's not the only thing to recover. I didn't want my spirit broken, too. I didn't want to be a different person than I was before the accident. I wasn't Superwoman, and I certainly still had my low moments, but rehab gave me some time to gradually grow more and more at peace with what I was dealing with. Also, I made a promise to myself that I was going to be fine.

I felt obligated to make sure everyone else was okay. I could see how the injury was affecting everyone around me. I wanted to lift them up in the same way I was working to lift myself up. Like a group project, almost, that I would lead. I convinced myself that it would all be fine. In going through that process in my head, I definitely put on a happy face for everyone else, I think because I needed to sort through it all. By being happy all the time, by telling jokes and laughing with other people, it helped me convince myself. It made it okay to believe because life felt normal. I think I had more support than many people have, but I also learned I was the most important support I'd need. I needed to know I could survive. I needed to know I was strong enough to get through. I needed to figure out in my head that, yes, this would all be okay.

In rehab Chris and I would always talk about how awesome my friends were and how lucky I was to have them in my life. We discussed how friends sometimes leave your side in these kinds of situations because they simply don't know how to handle them, and you often find out exactly who your real friends are. This was the case for me—it became clear to me what friendship stood for and what it meant. Suddenly, I knew I had true friends. There was no doubt in my mind that they would be there for me. Without them during those long months, it would have been harder to make it through. But they wouldn't have made it without me either; they told me that many times. We comforted each other and learned to be there for each other, and we started to really understand the impact that night had had on us as a group.

I had to heal. That was clear. But even more, I had to step up. I had to really be there for this girl, this friend who had pushed me in a simple, playful gesture. We laughed a lot, but I could see through our laughter. She hadn't even reached the low point of her despair during my rehab stint, though my friends and I didn't know this at the time. It was just an unspoken promise at this point that we all protected her instinctually. We acknowledged that the accident at the pool had happened but almost pretended that the push itself hadn't. Maybe we were in denial; maybe we weren't ready to open that can of worms just yet. It wasn't spoken, but it wasn't too far out of all of our minds. We focused on the recovery for sure. As I think back, it's almost like we refused to confront it. Whenever the thought of how I got where I was entered my mind, I'd push it out. If I didn't think about how the accident happened, then I didn't have to worry that our friendship would be different. But still waters run deep, and denial wasn't enough.

CHAPTER 14

Getting Through

About two months after the accident, I had my first intense conversation with that friend we were all so worried about. Everyone had been quietly thinking about her, hoping the worst had passed and she'd healed from what had happened. My brother had come out from Virginia Beach to stay with our family, and I learned that in the wake of the accident he had made a point to take her aside and tell her that I asked about her often and that I loved her. He wanted to make sure she was okay. We all did. I'd hoped it had been enough, laughing with her and having her see me in rehab really doing well.

There was a little garden area at the rehab center. It was always so freezing cold inside that I'd spend as much time as I could sitting out in this garden. It was hot out, around 100 degrees. I used to make people sit out there and stay with me, even though for them, it would have been more comfortable inside. My body had lost the ability to regulate its temperature, so I always felt cold. Some days, I simply could not stand being inside.

One afternoon, this friend was visiting. I had never brought up the incident because I didn't want to upset her. I knew she'd come talk to me when she was ready. And that day finally came.

Her face wasn't so much sad as it was very serious. We had made our way to the garden and she said, "I'm really sorry this happened." I think she just wanted to hear that I had forgiven her.

For me, it wasn't even about forgiveness. I'd have had to have thought that she did something really wrong to forgive her. She hadn't. It could have happened to anyone, and I didn't blame her.

She said, "I feel really bad about this. I'm so sorry."

I said, "Don't be and don't feel bad. I'm okay. I'm honestly at peace with it. You should be, too."

I had made peace with it in a very short amount of time. During this conversation I knew she had not yet found peace in the same way I had, but I thought she would soon. I was naive as to just how much she was hurting and how bad it was at that moment. I assumed that since I was okay, she'd be okay—that she just needed to hear me say I was all right.

She nodded. She was holding it together. "Are we okay?" she asked.

"Of course. I love you. You're one of my best friends. I don't blame you for this."

I thought, or maybe I hoped, that that would be enough. She didn't cry or break down, but deep down I guess she was putting on a good front. She was being strong for me, but she must have been hurting inside.

"When you're upset, talk to me. Call me. I will talk about this with you anytime," I said. I told her she didn't need to pay anyone to help her sort through her feelings, that I was there whenever she needed to speak, day or night. Maybe that was a mistake, but not really knowing how deeply affected she was, I suppose I believed she could shake it off. The problem was that we were accepting two different realities. We were both badly hurt that day, but in two completely different ways. I could work hard to make the best of my situation. She really couldn't. There was no upside to living with that hurt. There was no finding a way to put a bad situation to good use. It was just a tragic event that could have happened to any of us that night. I've had my share of horseplay in the water, that's for sure. Everyone has.

She thanked me that day, and I thought all was sorted out and we'd both be okay, leaning on each other for strength. Sadly, the worst was yet to come for her. She'd have to face this all later when the media circus began, which none of us saw coming.

CHAPTER 15

My Competitive Spirit

I WAS PRETTY ACTIVE AS A KID. WHEN I WAS GROWING UP, MY dad never just let me win a game. He allowed me to lose, and I wanted it that way. I was really good at board games, and I could usually win, even against my dad. Once though, he beat me at Pretty, Pretty Princess and he had to wear the crown and beads.

I loved sports and often played with my dad. He took me to basketball games as soon as I could walk. I liked to keep score, hug the mascots, and talk up the cheerleaders. We used to collect trading cards, too. Once, we were at a summer league game where prospective pros were scouted. My dad pointed out a player, Joe Smith, and told me he was going to be the number one draft pick. I was four years old at the time.

I said, "I want his autograph."

Instead of going to get it for me, my dad handed me a pen and a paper and said, "Go ask."

Of course I got it, but I was a little bummed not to have been treated like one of the guys by this player. He called me cute.

I think I always wanted to be one of the guys because I so loved hanging around my dad. During recess in fourth grade, I walked up to the boys and asked if I could shoot some hoops.

One said, "Girls can't play basketball." I made them give me the ball, took one shot, and swished it. After that I was always invited to play with them.

I worked with kids when I graduated from college, and we didn't even keep score until they were eight years old, because we didn't want the kids to get upset about losing. The thing is, if kids haven't ever lost until they are eight, how are they going to handle losing later in life? They will inevitably lose something. I knew when I had won. I knew when I had earned it. And I think that just made me more competitive. Not only that, I enjoyed working toward something. I really did. I enjoyed an accomplishment, however big or small.

Basketball was where my dad and I really bonded. On the court the winner won. He didn't allow me to get a free shot in, nothing. He made me work for everything, and I think I drew on that for strength after my accident. That was real life. You won some, you lost some. How you handled the ups and downs revealed your true character. Even when I was really little, my dad would never throw a game. People never believe me when I tell them that.

My dad and I would play the game Horse all the time, from when I was four until I was in high school. It was one of our things. We had a basketball hoop in the backyard and, as in everything else, he'd never let me win. He wouldn't go all pro player on me—he wasn't mean about it—but he played for real. I might get a few letters on him, but if I started catching up, then he'd up his effort and I'd lose. He'd just never *let me* win Horse. Never. Once when I was a teenager, I actually beat him at Horse—it was the one and only time. But it felt like the biggest accomplishment ever because it took me ten years to do it. The funny thing wasn't just my reaction, but his. He didn't like to be beaten, but he was so proud of me. He said, "You finally did it!" Of course, I couldn't help but shove it in his face and celebrate my sweet victory by talking some smack, but boy was I proud.

We were a sporty family, and we used to do a lot of activities together. We also played catch and football; I was kind of a tomboy when it came to that stuff. My dad worked sixty hours a week usually. But Sunday was our day. When spring hit we were outside on Sunday afternoons, playing sports.

Right after the accident, I was fighting as hard as I had fought in sports or games. I drew on that. I didn't want to break; I didn't want to lose the new battle. I guess I saw it as being weak, and I didn't like to be weak. Of course, no one would have blamed me for being crazy and breaking down and crying. But I saw it as a game I was trying to win, like I was trying to be the best at recovery. To have the best attitude.

This injury was almost like the Horse victory that was ten years in the making. I knew there were going to be little moments where I was going to have to suck it up and fight and beat those challenges. And I was determined to win.

Every time I lost at Horse, I didn't feel defeated. It made me feel more determined. I understood that it would be a miracle if I ever beat my dad at a game. I never expected to beat him, to be honest, but I always tried my hardest regardless. Being competitive at sports made me competitive at life, and this injury, well, I wanted to win. As I prepared to leave rehab, I drew on that inner fight and spirit my dad had spent a lifetime instilling in me.

Toward the end of rehab, my mom and I were in full prankster mode. I had a roommate in rehab, a lady who had worked at ECU. She had gone on a bike ride, fallen off the bike, and actually been stung by a bunch of bees. She broke her neck in the fall but ended up walking by the time she was out of treatment; she was an incomplete injury. It was so weird to see someone as paralyzed as I was, and then right before my eyes, see her walking. I think that happens a lot in rehab. I was definitely the most screwed-up one there at the time.

Anyway, her husband walked into the room one day, and my mom was in bum clothes, with no bra, so when she heard him coming, she opened the closet door to hide. It was like a dorm closet, a big cubbyhole with a door, so she opened the closet door very fast and fell into the closet and was basically sitting down. We were laughing so hard over the fact that she could fit into the closet, so I said, "Mom, stay in the closet." We called the nurse, Tammy. She came in and I said, "Tammy, I've got this beautiful dress, and I want to wear it out." (I was able to go on day trips once I was cleared, and my family could transfer me into a car. So I had been out in public by this time.) I told Tammy, "Look in my closet and get the dress out." She opened the door to find my mom just sitting there. Tammy screamed and threw a pillow at her, and we laughed hysterically.

Since Mom could sit in the closet, I wondered if I could, too. My mother checked. It was big enough to get a chair into, just a plastic chair. So this time we got Tammy on our side to scare the doctor. Tammy happily got in on our scheme and a couple of therapists did, too. The night before our prank, I practiced how I would fit, and it totally worked. And then the next day we scared some more people. We spent the day, my last day at the rehab hospital, using this trick. I remained in the closet while Tammy or a therapist brought someone by. Tammy was so funny because she'd have to create elaborate lies to get people to open the closet. She told my caseworker I was hoarding catheters. She told the supply guy that I'd stolen a box of medical gloves. She even told the doctors I was stashing medication in that closet.

That was the day I left and got to go home. Everyone had made such a significant impression on me and my life during my time there. They were such wonderful people. I guess I'm glad the closet gag gave me the chance to leave an impression on them . . . and maybe let them know I'd be okay once I left their care because I had a good sense of humor and was surrounded by a lot of love.

CHAPTER 16

On My Own

I LEFT REHAB ON AUGUST 13, 2010. I HAD SO MANY MIXED FEELINGS about leaving. I knew I was ready to go, and I remember around the time I was being released thinking that if I had to stay there one more minute, I would snap. There were so many people there with lower-level injuries who had more function than I did, people recovering quickly, and they complained often; sometimes the negative energy took the wind out of me. I had reached the point where I simply couldn't take it anymore. I felt for everyone and didn't mean to judge. Not everyone had a great network of friends or a committed family, and I understood that. But sometimes the negative energy consumed the space in there. An exciting world still existed out there, and I was more eager to tackle the new challenges than to dwell on what I couldn't do. I wanted to learn and grow and take it on. Also, I missed my dog PeeDee very much. I missed my house and my old life, which I knew was going to be at home waiting for me.

Of course, that's what terrified me, too. Just because I was okay with challenges didn't mean they weren't scary. My old life was just that: my old life. Nothing was the same except my love for Chris and my family and friends. I knew I wouldn't be able to get up to the second floor to my bedroom. The house was my home, but it was no longer what it had once been to me. I had been there only as an able-bodied person. There would be a lot of change ahead of me. All of my care would be up to us, and lots of little things could go wrong.

One of the most significant changes in my life was that my mother would have to live with us. Chris had to go to work, and my mother had to get me out of bed. I was thrilled, but I realized it would be a tremendous hardship for her, leaving her job and her husband. We all thought about me moving in with them, but that would have kept me from both Chris and rehab. We discussed briefly both of my parents moving to Knightdale, but my dad had an army-navy surplus store in Norfolk and couldn't leave it. We knew eventually he'd sell it and retire, but until then my mother decided to spend five days a week with me and weekends with my dad.

It was hard for her, but she moved in without complaining. We knew we all had to change our lives drastically, and I appreciated that she agreed to change hers as well. I knew when I returned home from rehab that I'd continue to see my friends, go to ECU football games eventually, and eat at the restaurant that I always went to. I was able to come back to my house and be in my own environment with the people I cared about. So, in a sense, I did return to my life, but she couldn't. We decided as I left rehab that hopefully one year or so would be enough to get me settled.

I knew then that I could manage only halfway on my own. If I wanted to wear sweatpants and a T-shirt every day, I could put that on myself. I hadn't learned to transfer from my bed to my chair and wasn't sure if I ever would, so my mom would have to get me out of bed and up every day. I knew having her there would make things feel as normal as possible for me, and I was grateful for her sacrifice and willingness to play my unsung hero. I learned the true meaning of friendship from my mother. She was my best friend growing up, and she set the tone for all of my other relationships.

I realized quickly that caring for me was emotionally draining for her. In addition to needing help moving, there were serious medical complications that plagued me, and seeing me struggle upset my mother terribly. She had to always be on high alert, because we realized quickly that my blood pressure dropped so low that there were days when I had a hard time keeping my head up without passing out.

I also suffered from severe nerve pain, which was an unexpected yet overwhelming side effect. On a normal day I would spend a good hour getting out of bed, because I had to wait for the nerve pain to go away. This pain doesn't happen to everyone, and there's no explanation as to why it happens in some with spinal cord injuries and not in others. Mine in particular was pretty debilitating, occurring mostly when I woke up but lessening during the day. In the early morning movement was impossible. Nerve pain feels like fire, it feels like needles, it feels like beatings all over, or even like a thousand bees stinging me all at once. Basically, wherever I had no normal feeling is where I would have this nerve pain, everywhere from my chest down. My brain would try to connect with my body. When it was unable to, it would send a signal back in the form of pain.

The nerve pain was one of the harshest realities of my injury, and I was told I would likely live with it forever. It gradually became a part of my life, increasing bit by bit each day. It became worse when the weather deteriorated, and some days it grew unbearable. If I had known how bad it was going to be, and how overwhelming the pain, I never would have survived this experience. Initially, I felt upset because I learned it was a rarity—very few people with a spinal cord injury experience my level of pain. Whenever I mentioned it to other friends in a chair, they all told me it was something they'd gotten used to, which indicated to me that we were not talking about the same pain. This was not a tingling "sensation." It was absolute torture. If you asked me, "Would you rather walk again, but live with the nerve pain, or stay in the wheelchair and be pain free?" I would choose the latter.

I remember the first few times it happened, I was screaming as I was awakened by the pain. I could hear my mother sobbing in the other room, upset that I was suffering. I felt so badly for her. I tried multiple pain-relieving meds, but none seemed to work. It was frightening because the main one I took would essentially destroy my life over time, which made me realize it would have been nice not to be on any meds at all; I couldn't be sure that they were even helping me or having a positive impact.

My mother and I dealt with logistical issues, too, once home. Once, on a really hot day, my mother was trying to get me into the car, and I fell on the hot pavement in the driveway. She couldn't lift me because I was too heavy. I was in shorts, lying there, and she started to panic. She thought my legs would burn on the hot asphalt. I said to her, "This is not the time to panic. I'm okay." She ran into the garage, found a very low-rise lawn chair, and managed to get me into it. I had some scrapes on my knees but really nothing major.

The other issue we knew we'd face out of rehab, which was a major concern, was that if we had any kind of problem medically, and we did occasionally, we'd have to go to a doctor or hospital. There was no longer a nurse's button to press for help. There wasn't all this great equipment, or fast diagnoses, or people checking up on me all the time. It was on us. Period.

Very few local places had experts on spinal cord injuries. A couple of months after I returned home, I had an incident that sent me to the emergency room. When I was in the hospital recovering, at least I knew there were people around to help. But when I was home, it was scary when something went wrong. In order to go to the bathroom, I had to insert a catheter, and one day when I did that, there was all this blood. I had no idea what was going on. I was dizzy, and my body was reacting badly. My mother and I were alone, and we didn't know what to do. Normally, at the hospital, we'd call a nurse in, but we were on our own, and I couldn't even sit up enough to get into the car and go to the hospital. We had to call an ambulance. So I had to have EMS come to the house and put me on a stretcher, because I was so dizzy. I had an infection, and my body had to tell me in a different way than another person's body would tell her. I was extremely lightheaded, and my blood pressure was sky-high. It was a traumatic moment. I was thinking, *This is not supposed to be my life. I am not supposed to have EMS coming to my house and getting me.* It was a moment when I had to suck it up and fight through it.

It turned out it was a really bad bladder infection. For an uninjured woman it would hurt like crap, and she would know something was wrong early on and of course go to the doctor, get some medication, and clear it up. But for me it was different because I couldn't feel anything. An infection wouldn't alert me with pain. My body had to react in a different way. I got clammy and sweaty, had goose bumps, and felt dizzy. They were all signs that something was wrong with my body.

These were symptoms of autonomic dysreflexia, which affects people with spinal cord injuries like mine. Because I was hurt at a higher level of injury, my autonomic nervous system was also affected. If I had been hurt below a T-7, which is someone paralyzed only from the rib-cage area down, then my autonomic nervous system would have been intact. My blood pressure would have been normal, I would have sweated regularly, and so on. But when there was pain in my body and something went wrong, my nervous system reacted and my blood pressure shot up. I got goose bumps, felt sort of clammy, and had the shakes. I could die if I didn't figure out what was wrong quickly. I could wind up dying from a urinary tract infection because my blood pressure increased so dramatically.

I was lucky that I experienced it only twice. Some people get it all the time. If I was wearing pants with a zipper on them and they were poking into me, I'd become really dizzy and I'd have to look at my body and try to determine what was wrong. It was scary because I couldn't feel anything from my chest down, so numerous things could be the cause—it was a large area!

One weekend, Lauren came to visit and stay with me. My mom was like a second mom to her, so we all hung out together all weekend. She caught a real glimpse into the reality of my injury. Chris was still carrying me up the stairs on his back at that point, as the house hadn't been updated yet, and since I was cold all the time, I had to sit near the heater. She'd heard all about this from the other girls, but seeing it was different. We had a really fun Saturday, all of us, going out to eat and laughing, but on Sunday, before Lauren even woke up, my mother and I had to go to the hospital because I had another UTI. Lauren called us when she woke up, and it seemed like we were going to be at the emergency room for hours and hours, so she headed back to Charlotte.

I think it was an eye-opener for her, seeing the day-to-day. She did get to see me play quad rugby, which was cool, and we did hang out, but the reality of it all wasn't lost on her. She even told me later that her life's mindset was different after that, that her perspective on life and enjoying it was so altered—she appreciated everything she had so much more. And her love of our other friends was strong and genuine. She told me she was speaking to one of the other girls once, and that girl said she was going to run, to use her legs as much as possible, to honor me. I thought that was pretty cool. I know each of the girls handled and processed the accident differently.

CHAPTER 17

Adjusting at Home

THE PROCESS OF GETTING OUT OF BED EVERY MORNING TOOK ABOUT an hour once I refined it. It took up to two hours when I first got home, but we managed to figure out how to make it quicker. The pain and dizziness slowed things down considerably, but on a good day, when my mom dressed me in the morning, we'd get that part down to ten minutes. Since I have some arm use, I could have slid a top on fairly quickly, but pants would have taken me about forty-five minutes to get into. My mother sped that up considerably, so it made sense for her to start helping me dress.

Sleeping was a big challenge, which I hadn't expected. Like anyone, if I were up all night, which happened with great frequency, the morning would be rough. I couldn't roll over or change positions. When I first returned home, my mother and Chris would turn me over in the middle of the night. There was initial concern I'd get bedsores from not being able to move. Chris would go to work wiped out from not getting continuous rest, so they eventually switched off and let him turn me only on weekends. After a few months they weaned me off of this process and I didn't get pressure sores at all. I missed being able to roll over and wrap myself around Chris. I compensated for that by cherishing his touch. Sometimes, when I was awake at night, I'd look down to see his hand on my hip. It made me feel safe seeing it, knowing he was embracing me, even if I couldn't feel it.

The entire situation was exhausting for everyone, especially my mom. We had to figure out how to dress me, book and keep track of appointments, and transport me to those appointments. It was an enormous undertaking, and we didn't know what we were doing. One morning, after my mother helped me out of bed, dressed me, and everything else, at a time when we were still getting our routine down, she was styling my hair for me. I asked her to spray hairspray on me, and she was so tired and frazzled that she sprayed Pine-Sol on my hair instead. She had my hair perfect, too. She was so distracted that she soaked it in cleaning supplies. We had to redo it, but we laughed so hard at what had happened, we cried.

It was difficult to keep up with the clutter, too. I loved a clean house, and I was frustrated at first with all the medical supplies stacked up in my bedroom. I think that impacted my sleeping a little.

My friends were so amazing during this time. They all wanted to help and give my mother a reprieve. Carly used to make it over twice a month to hang out and keep me company. While she was there she helped take some of the responsibility off of my mom by cathing me. It had to be done four times a day. I threw the bag away as it filled. This duty had the potential to be upsetting, but it was mostly humorous when she took the first couple of shots at it. We laughed about it a lot, about how we couldn't imagine two years ago that one of us would be seeing me from this angle. She also knew how to transfer me, lifting me up onto my chair. She was great company and gave my mother some much-needed relief.

My brother, Aaron, was a big help as well. For the first six months, he moved from Virginia Beach to North Carolina to live with me. He was able to pick me up and put me on the couch, and it relieved my mom a bit from having to do everything.

We wound up actually making a crazy connection through some serious talks, which became fairly deep. Once when we were sitting up at night on the couch, he said, "I thought the world was kind of a cruel place. I thought it was filled with only selfish people. I have a different outlook now, after seeing so many people who care about you, stepping up."

He saw my friends, my parents, Chris, even strangers who donated time and energy and goods and money that changed my life, and he was moved. He hadn't realized people could be like that. He was jaded before I was injured. The accident had actually restored his faith in people. When I heard things like that, it made the injury feel easier, as if there was an upside to it. I had pain and suffering, sure, but I grabbed hold of moments like this with my brother, these little enlightening revelations, and it kept me going.

Aaron stayed with us until we managed to restore a sense of order, and then he moved in with our friend Tom, who was close by. It was really nice to have Aaron near us. One time he was over at the house hanging out, and my mom stepped out for a little while. I was still in bed. I can't remember what I dropped, but whatever it was it must have made him think I had fallen out of bed. Three seconds later, he threw open the door.

Startled, I said, "Well, hello there."

He said, "That was so loud I thought you fell."

We laughed so hard. He must have hit only three steps of the full staircase, he moved so quickly.

I felt like I didn't really know him very well before the accident. Maybe my entire life. He was eight years older, so we never hung out. But after the accident we became extremely close. He lived down the street and came over for dinner, and I saw him much more than when we were young. I was grateful for renewing that connection. It was awesome just to be able to chill with him in a way that I hadn't expected.

CHAPTER 18

The Ugly Reality

UNFORTUNATELY, WHILE I WAS GETTING USED TO THINGS INSIDE OF my home, factors I couldn't control outside of my home painted an unexpected picture of how people with spinal cord injuries are sometimes treated. Ugly truths began to reveal themselves to me, and I was shocked by some of my experiences.

I'd never really given parking much thought, but when my mother started driving me around, we soon realized that accessible spaces were scarce and that few people respected the law. I even began to think about the name *handicap parking* and why it was still socially acceptable. The term *handicap* originated in a time when people who were in wheelchairs and couldn't work would have to put a hat out for money, or a "handi-cap." Many people don't know that history, and when they say that word, they don't mean anything by it.

My first run-in with the issue was when I still had a neck brace on, and at that point I had no idea that people abuse handicap parking spots the way they do. A guy on a motorcycle had parked between the lines of two handicap spots; usually that space is reserved for a ramp to come out. Regardless, I don't know why anyone would park there; obviously someone could come out of their car in a wheelchair, and anyone thinking logically would know that they needed space to do so.

I was in my mother's car, and I had to be slide-boarded out of it. My mom had to get in front of me to slide me out of the car. The guy had parked so close. Now, I was a confident person, but I did not want to be dragged out of a car like a ragdoll with a neck brace right in front of some idiot because he was too stubborn to move. It just was not a comfortable situation. I remember my mom asking him very nicely to move. He said, "All right," and then all he did was bring his leg around to the other side of his motorcycle. This guy didn't even look me in the eye, didn't make any space for me to get out. He was such an asshole. He just sat there, right next to our car—one foot away from my wheelchair. A waitress came out, and he sat there flirting with her while I was struggling with my mom to get out of the car and into my chair. I said to my mother out loud, "Is this really happening?" We were boiling mad, since it was so soon after the accident and we hadn't encountered anyone quite so obnoxious and selfish. I should have said more. I wasn't afraid of him or even nervous, but until that point, I just had not known people acted like that. He could clearly see I was sitting in the car with a neck brace and a wheelchair, and he needed to get out of the way and he wouldn't. I thought, *Just get out of the way. Period.* It boggled my mind. Of course, just as I was out and in the chair, he took off, revving up the bike really loudly and speeding away. He couldn't even walk his motorcycle out four feet. He had to start it next to us like that.

The next time that happened, I had more smarts and awareness. We went back to the same restaurant, which attracts a lot of sporty people and people with motorcycles. A man had parked his motorcycle *on the lines of* the handicap spot. So I waited. I knew I couldn't walk away from everyone who abused these things; otherwise I was not doing anything to better the situation. If I spoke up, maybe an able-bodied driver wouldn't do it again, and maybe the next injured person wouldn't have a hard time coming out of his or her car. I realized that the more people I could educate, the fewer injured people would face what I was facing right then.

So we waited and waited for this one guy; it was a frustrating experience. I eventually called the cops this time, and the cop was totally on my side. The guy finally emerged from the restaurant, and he noticed the cop by his motorcycle.

He said, "I was only there for one minute." That's everyone's excuse, by the way.

I said, "That's not true. I called the cops twenty minutes ago."

The cop said I was right.

So the cop made the guy come over and apologize to me, but then the cop apologized to me because he couldn't write the guy a ticket. The guy wasn't technically *in* the handicap spot. He was in the wide space between the two painted lines that separated it from another parking space, the space to create room for people in wheelchairs to get out between the cars. I tried to argue that parking on the line made the handicap spot inaccessible and invalid, essentially. The lines are part of the spot and illegal to park on. I was happy the cop wanted to stand up for me, but clearly he didn't understand the law. The cop said to me, "I will get him for something else." And he did. The guy didn't have the correct helmet and so he couldn't ride off. He was livid and had to walk his bike home. Still, it wasn't enough.

CHAPTER 19

The Pact

IN NOVEMBER CHRIS AND I GRADUALLY BEGAN RECEIVING A LOT OF press about our love story and the accident. While some incredible things emerged from that exposure, it was a doubled-edged sword. It exposed the friend who had playfully pushed me to some unexpected nastiness and brought all of the feelings from that night bubbling up to the surface. The unexpected bad part happened over the use of one word, really rocking her world. It was a report that used the word *prank*. This headline changed everything for my friend: WORST BRIDESMAID PRANK EVER LEAVES BRIDE PARAPLEGIC AND UNMARRIED. It almost seemed as if some outlets were only interested in overdramatizing my story and not concerned about getting the facts straight. It's not as if the story required any more drama. In the same news broadcast that called it a prank, they said the pool was two feet deep. They had even called to clarify with me before airing the story, and I had told them the shallow end was four feet deep. By making it worse than it already was, it just gave people more negative things to say about her and the entire situation. Some stories even said I was thrown in. What a big difference one word made.

She had come to watch me play at a quad rugby tournament, along with two other girls from the pool that night. After the match they were in my hotel room, and we knew the story would be on, so we watched on the computer. That was the start of her really having to confront what had happened that night. She couldn't deny her feelings anymore because everything about that night was now public knowledge, and she was a central character in the entire ordeal. The denial she was perhaps using to cope ultimately only masked her true heartache, which none of us had seen fully up to that point.

As soon as she heard it, I knew immediately that the word *prank* would bother her. It was a terrible, dumb word, but I didn't know what kind of impact it would have. It was a really poor choice that left me feeling rubbed the wrong way. I was unaware how much it would dig into her. We talked about it. She told me that the moment she heard it, she was upset, and that the next day she still couldn't shake it. She said, "They called it a prank. It wasn't a prank." She was extremely upset. She obviously had lost sleep over this report. We all knew this was going to be a problem for her and that it was going to snowball from there.

I received a hard lesson in the importance of language. After hearing *prank,* which I never would have said myself, I was much more aware of my word choice and how what I said would be portrayed. I made it a point then to start using the term *playfully pushed,* and some of the media actually caught on.

Unfortunately, others began doing stories and the word *prank* gathered momentum. It became the more frequently used word to describe the night. My friend broke down. That word crushed her. She tried to hold on, but once the national media latched on to the story, her pain escalated.

Just as the story started to spread, she came to me. It was like she was falling off a cliff in front of me, and I couldn't stop her.

"I can see that you're hurting," she said. "I feel like I don't deserve to be happy and I don't deserve to have a good life." The floodgates had been holding back all of her emotion, but that one word opened them up, and it all rushed out in front of us at once. I was saddened and surprised she'd been holding on to the guilt and anxiety.

I begged her to really understand that I wasn't hurting. I was having bad days and good ones, sure, but a bad event didn't take over my life, and I was making more than the most of it. I was rising above the challenge, and I was strong and happy as a result.

All of the girls from that night by the pool were athletic. They ran, played sports, swam. That was part of our bond. She said, "When I'm out doing something active, using my legs, I feel guilty."

I told her not to even think about it, just to enjoy it, that it was okay. I told her, "Be active for me." I wanted all of my friends to live life like it was their last day. Most tried, but with her it just wouldn't sink in, and that word wouldn't go away. *Prank.* It was the most evil trigger for her.

The media attention that followed overwhelmed me and became a part of my everyday life. In all of this, I was never really angry about my situation, but one thing did infuriate me: the way people spoke of my poor friend. It was awful and unrelenting. People would comment on stories, saying horrible things. Nonstop.

Forget how insulting it was to me; my friend was devastated because the word *prank* made it sound like she had planned the push and it was on purpose, and that really wasn't how it happened at all. Notice that whoever wrote the original headline and story didn't even get the simple facts correct—I'm a quadriplegic, not a paraplegic.

Then there were the thousands of comments in the thread of that particular story. People said terrible things about Chris and sometimes about me, such as, "Don't have children with her because you'll have to raise them yourself." But we let it slide. My friend couldn't let it go so easily. One person commented, "I'm sure the friend feels terrible and she should. She crippled this woman because she didn't think." Aside from the fact that the word *crippled* was incredibly offensive and demonstrated tremendous ignorance, the writer of such scathing statements had no idea how my friend or any of us felt.

I wanted to scream, really, at the stupidity of it all. It could have happened to absolutely anyone. It's not uncommon to put a light hand on someone and give them a tender shove into the pool. I've done it. The people writing these comments, they must have led some seriously perfect lives and had really good luck. There were of course multiple supportive comments, but they didn't even cause a blip on my friend's radar. They were eclipsed by the nasty, evil ones that had so much impact.

The accident just happened. It was scary and random, but to write that she should be crippled, too? It was just plain insanity and judgmental, and I hoped none of these people ever had to deal with this situation, because that was no way to find peace. No one is immune to an accident. All of us have done things in our lives that could have caused injury.

People asked me all of the time if I was angry about the accident. The only time I felt anger about this accident was when I read crap like this. It was never-ending. I knew I shouldn't read it all, but I couldn't help myself.

My friend started reading it all, too, more and more. I don't know why. But then she began believing it. Even after I was long out of the hospital and on the road to figuring out my life, she kept getting stuck on the negativity, and with every story she felt worse and worse. People wrote that she should hurt herself, or she should be paralyzed, too, and indebted to me. They got inside her head. These evil, rotten people really messed with her.

Early on she was so consumed by it all, worried that people would figure out who she was, that she stopped using Facebook and shut down in other ways, too. We all sort of closed out of Facebook for a while. She decided if she posted anything to me, she was giving it away that she'd pushed me, even by posting a picture. She didn't want anyone to know anything. I respected that fear and never talked about it at all, not a word.

At one point *In Touch* magazine became really aggressive, trying to figure out who was there that night and who had pushed me into the pool. They actually went so far as to contact about one hundred people on Facebook who were friends with me, trying to put the pieces together. I had casually spoken with the other girls all along about how protective we needed to be of our friend's feelings. We all agreed that had the situation been reversed, it would be painful to feel responsible, and in an unspoken way, we all respected and protected that. But the *In Touch* situation was upsetting. It meant it was time to draw a line in the sand. We had to formalize things. I phoned each girl individually and said, "That's it. We aren't going to talk about it." No one argued, that's for sure, and we made a promise to protect ourselves as a group and to protect our friend who had been the most emotionally devastated by the traumatic event. It was a pivotal moment. The pact had been unspoken until that point, but we knew we were stronger as a whole than we were on our own, so we all agreed it was us against them. I called her, too, and told her that we promised this secret would never get out.

After that, my friend who was having a hard time with the accident began to call me daily, and during our talks she would always apologize profusely. The media blitz intensified, and she appeared to sink deeply during the day. During every call I'd tell her about all the great things that were happening. By the time we hung up, it felt like she was hearing it and it was sinking in. I soon realized that the lift was always temporary, and that by the next day, her despair would reemerge. I felt so sad for her and was deeply concerned. I could tell that a one-second event had really bled into her being. I think she distracted herself at work, but in quiet moments it was harder on her. I could relate; it was like that for me in rehab.

Eventually, I began to worry our friendship might never be the same. I did not want the accident to get in the way of what would have been a fun-filled girly visit, like the ones we had shared before the accident, but it did. The accident loomed large. Up until then I really thought each and every day she'd turned the corner. One afternoon, seeing me in the wheelchair at my home really upset her. It was before we had had the place remodeled and was the first time she'd visited me there, when it was more difficult for me to get around. Someone had carried me upstairs before her arrival, but I had no way to get down on my own. That meant that she and I would have to stay up there together for the entire day. She hadn't seen how limited I was before that day. She had to experience what I was living, and she really felt it.

At first we tried to make casual conversation, but it was strained. It was awkward and forced. I wouldn't say the visit was fun; it was uncomfortable. Not that I was uncomfortable being around her—it just felt sucky being with a great friend with this accident looming there between us. She was hiding what she was feeling, I think for both our sakes. She didn't want me to feel bad for her, and she didn't want to face all that was happening. I feared she hadn't even admitted to herself how much pain she was in. She was a pretty strong-willed person; she and I were alike in that sense. She was putting on a brave face for me, but there had been a lot of denial. I think she just pushed it all down at the beginning. I knew she had guilt, but I thought she could manage it. Maybe she even ignored the stress of what it was doing to her and just thought it would go away.

So at the end of this long, weird day, Chris, my mom, his parents, my friend, and I were going to a restaurant for dinner. It was the Lone Star Steakhouse near my house. It was my favorite restaurant, and I was excited we were all going. I loved steak, and their rolls were so good. But that night, I became so cold from the air-conditioning that I began shivering, and it actually made me feel dizzy. I felt so awful that I had to leave before dinner was over. Chris put me in my friend's car and went back in to finish eating, and my friend and I sat there for a while so I could feel better. Then we decided to go to Burger King. She didn't say much. She just experienced it with me but didn't really know what to do. I remember feeling so bad at the time that she had to see how it all played out. I didn't want to show her the weakness of the injury. I didn't want her to see it in my everyday life. But I knew it had hurt her.

One very intense conversation between us was laced with both positive and negative. *Today* had been great about getting my story out there, and *Headline News* had, too. After my appearances on these programs, some wonderful things were sent in that really helped me. People sent money through a special-needs trust I had set up, and it was enough to pay for a monthly insurance premium for a year or two. A team from the show *George to the Rescue* remodeled my home, making it wheelchair friendly, and Lulus.com donated some clothes to help me feel beautiful. But there was a flip side to the publicity.

"What do these people really want from me?" my friend asked about the media outlets that seemed to sensationalize the accident in their reports.

"Ignore them. We are. We're never letting them in," I tried to assure her.

She said, "I hope you know, I'm happy for all the good that is coming of this and all the great things you're doing as a result."

"Thank you. I know you are," I said. "There's a lot of cool stuff going on, and I'm psyched."

Then we got back to the undercurrent of it all. "Why are they coming after me? Do you think they'll figure it out?"

"We won't let them, I promise."

"I'm afraid of what people will do and say if they find out it was me," she said.

By the end of it that day, as with most days we spoke, she seemed fine. She seemed upbeat, and she could see I was invigorated by the positive elements of my story being told and all the nice letters and words I was receiving from people. She left that night, and I thought she was going to be okay. But then the next day, and then many of the following days and weeks, we'd talk and it was strained. There was a lot of "How are you?" but not much else. It felt as if our friendship was a shadow of what it used to be like. We wanted to talk more, I knew that much. We wanted to be genuine, but we were trying to avoid getting into the discussion of my injury. So it was always weird, and while generally it ended with her feeling better, the next day the negative feelings crept back in.

I never told her, but as she bottomed out right after that first *Today* interview, I became really concerned. The shift in her stress was visible. I was worried that if her name was revealed, she might do something bad to herself, like commit suicide. It just felt like it was that overwhelming to her, and she was that worried about it all. The requests for interviews and evil comments with her name in them would have been too much. She was good at putting on a smile, but I could see through her. She didn't want me to hear her cry, but the spunk was out of her voice. It was timid. She was not at all her usual strong-willed, vibrant self. That's why I continued and will always continue to protect her. I knew the stakes were high.

CHAPTER 20

Turning Down Oprah

OBVIOUSLY, THE ACCIDENT HAD BEEN DIFFICULT FOR MY FRIEND to deal with. It was tough for all of us. The other girls were always reminded and their lives changed, too. Mine had radically changed, but so much good was coming from it all that I was getting carried along by the momentum. I thought, eventually, she would simply figure it all out in her head and find peace. But with so many people trying to interject and get her story, and all the horrible comments that she couldn't help but read, it just became unbearable for her. She was terrified of the online bullying that would likely occur if they found her out. It had been bad enough without her name out there.

I remember sitting at home one afternoon in January and receiving an e-mail from a producer for Oprah Winfrey. I was so excited. I was a little mystified, too. Oprah Winfrey? I mean, I knew my story was interesting to people, but I was surprised it was *that* interesting. I'd watched Oprah almost every day. She was my idol. I knew this was something I needed to share with my friend, so I gave her a call. I thought that good news for me would make her feel good, too, that she'd see these really cool things happening for me and be relieved in a way. But I also knew the attention on my story made her nervous.

"Oprah wants to talk to me!" I said.

"That's cool," she said. I could tell she was a little anxious. "Are they going to want to talk about me?" she asked sheepishly.

"Of course not. Oprah would never ask that." I thought Oprah wanted to hear about my love story and have Chris and me appear on the show together. "Don't even give it a thought. I can't imagine that's what they want, but it doesn't matter because even if they do, I wouldn't do anything to hurt you. So don't worry about it."

I finally did speak to a producer and my heart just sank. A few people had wanted the story, but I had been clear that I wasn't going to say anything about my friend. *Oprah* was really the last outlet I thought would ask because that information had been more of a quest of the tabloids and gossip magazines up to this point.

"We're doing a show on forgiveness...." That was all I needed to hear. I explained to her that I don't look at it like something I need to forgive. If someone had hurt me intentionally, then forgiveness would be in order. But there was no ill intent. I would have had to have been angry in order to forgive, and I wasn't. There was no blame, so nothing to forgive. I didn't even consider asking my friend to participate. The thought never even occurred to me.

I said, "I can't do that to her. She can't talk about it. She doesn't talk to anyone about what happened. It hurts too much."

It turned out the producer wanted us both to come on the show. She told me it would happen only if I brought my friend along. I think she was stunned we'd turn down Oprah—that anyone would turn down Oprah. She called back twice, asking me to appear with my friend, trying to convince me, pressing harder each time. Twice more I said no. I offered to come alone, but they weren't interested. I explained that my friend was having serious anxiety attacks and that it would be too much for me even to ask her.

A lot of people have asked me and the other girls there that night why we were so protective. Seriously? Releasing her identity would have been equivalent to releasing the hounds, so to speak. We would have been an accessory to her pain. What human being would do that to another person? I know her better than anyone, I think. I know it would break her if I didn't continue to protect her and hide her identity. If people hadn't been so evil and mean with comments and seeking out her name, we might never have needed to work so hard to shield her. We might have been able to go on *Oprah* and discuss our friendship. It was unfortunately made apparent early on that we had to step in and form our protective pact; people were suggesting online some seriously inhumane things. We couldn't stand for that.

The *Oprah* folks acted like an appearance on the show would help her heal, but I felt they didn't have our best interests at heart. It would have ruined all of us, and we all knew that. What if her name was out there and people could message her directly, before she'd had a chance to heal? We knew the risk was too great. That's what bothered me the most about Oprah's people. How could someone who had no idea who I was or who she was try to convince me this was good for us? Believe me, it was Oprah, and I was starry-eyed. But not stupid. I was offended that they tried to coax me like I was an idiot. I felt disillusioned. I idolized Oprah. I grew up watching her. I thought Oprah would do the same thing for her friend, too. I thought Oprah would have been proud of how I was taking a stand for a friend's life and well-being. I think had she actually known that, she herself would have understood. She is famous for being a tremendous friend. I was being a pillar of strength at my weakest moment to help someone in a worse predicament. I knew Oprah would have appreciated that act. At least, I hope.

I wound up having the same conversation over and over with my friend with great frequency after that. It appeared to hit her hardest right then. I remember my words, on the phone or if she'd come to visit. It was always the same.

"You don't deserve to feel anything from this," I'd explain.

I'd say, "I've pushed you in the pool so many times; you've pushed me in. It's just this one time I got hurt. It doesn't make me better, and it doesn't make you a bad person that this happened this time. We've messed around near the water before."

She would call when she was anxious, but the calls started to dwindle a bit. She would feel better when we hung up, that I could tell, but it seemed it would all creep back in overnight and she'd wake up the next day stressed again. She never told me she was going to kill herself, but it became a growing fear of mine as the media barrage escalated and the risk of her name getting out grew. I felt like it would be a very long road to her finding happiness, if that even happened. I felt like I'd lose my control of the situation if her name got out there. I don't think I would have been able to pull her back from the damage that would have done.

I knew she was trying to stay busy with her work. She had a great job, and all of us were there for her. I comforted her the most, I thought, because when she could see I was okay, then she felt okay. "I'm at peace. You should be, too." I told her again and again, "Don't waste your money paying to talk to someone you don't know." It seemed like it was the right thing. A therapist would cost so much money, and even though she had insurance and had toyed with the idea, I thought I could help her more, that I'd get the words right, that I'd comfort her because it had happened to us, not a stranger. I worried that once-a-week sessions wouldn't be enough, and that she'd maybe shift away from talking to me. I didn't want to manage the situation in a control-freak kind of way, but I wanted to offer some sort of control for her. I knew it would take her so long to develop trust with a stranger but that we already had deep trust between us. Even as I told her I could be her support again and again, maybe at that point she should have spoken to someone. Maybe it was too much for her and I wasn't equipped. She fell into such a blue place. Maybe a therapist could have helped her. That was one regret I did have as months went by and she didn't appear to feel better.

CHAPTER 21

Laughter and Tears

CARLY AND SAMANTHA WERE SERIOUSLY FUNNY GIRLS. ONE DAY, about a year after the accident, they'd come with me to my rugby tournament. It was my first season of rugby, and as we went to the gym Carly was wheeling me through double open doors. As we were approaching, I said, "Hey, you see that thing in the middle where the doors close? Watch out for that."

Carly said, "Okay."

She must have thought my wheelchair could go over it, but my footplate was too low, and so when she went head on into it, the chair stopped but I didn't. I fell out of the chair and flew through the air. Both girls tried to reach down and catch me by my sweatshirt, but that didn't work; they couldn't get a grip at all. It happened in slow motion. Well, I was lying there on the floor, not hurt, and none of us could stop laughing. That kind of situation always made me laugh. It reminded me a bit of life before the accident, because it was the kind of crazy stuff we used to laugh about back then, too. It was a cool moment because there was always stress about the accident and me being in a wheelchair, but this was just a good old-fashioned laugh, and it felt great. It wasn't scary. People fall out of their chairs all the time.

Something else fell out another time shortly after that, but it wasn't my entire body. It was my boob. One night, Samantha, Carly, and I went to dinner. It was the first time I'd gone out without Chris or my mother to help with the transition out of a car. We pulled up to the valet parking guy, which was our only option, and began the process of getting me out. We were laughing hysterically because it took both of them to slide me out of the car to go into the restaurant. The valet guy just stood at first, but when he saw them struggling, he tried to get in there and help. But one of my boobs had popped out of my dress, so of course we were laughing even harder at this point, and there was chaos because they were trying to get him to go away while they stuffed my boob back in the dress. They worked hard not to drop me on the ground. We caused quite a scene before they got me into my chair to go eat.

With no plans yet to set a wedding date and the media coverage continuing, there seemed to be little improvement for my one friend in getting beyond the accident. In one of our daily calls, she said, "It's really hard to see you like this. I don't want this to cause distance between us just because it's hard for me. Please don't let this happen. Call me every day."

"I won't let us slip," I said. "I'm here for you."

"I'm afraid I'll put myself somewhere away from you," she admitted. I knew seeing me was a constant reminder of her agony. Both of us knew we didn't want to lose a friend. Sometimes it is human nature to run away from what scares you, to distance yourself from something that might unleash bad memories.

I think she had the urge to push herself away from me to feel better, but she was asking me to help her stay strong. In part, she felt like she didn't deserve to be my friend anymore, but she wanted to. She wanted to heal. I know that.

I missed talking about boys and going out and life. Our conversations were always the same now, so repetitive. I wanted so badly for my words to stick.

"I don't have any nerve pain today," I'd tell her. Or, "I had a really good day today," or "I got a great letter today." I would relate anything positive that happened. You could hear her breathing change either in person or on the phone. Literally. It was that important to make her feel better.

She would get it. She would get that I was happy. She would get that I had moved on. Everyone else had. The family had. We drew on the great things that had happened. We wanted to grab her and shake her and pull her in on all of the joy we felt.

She had become severely depressed. She kept saying that if people knew it was her, they would have been calling for interviews and she wasn't ready to talk about it. I honestly felt she would have been viciously slandered in the media, and she didn't deserve that. People were so judgmental, as if they'd never made a mistake: never taken their eyes off the road for a split second to change the radio station, never accidentally run a red light, never been part of horseplay or fooled around. Something bad had happened as the result of an innocent gesture, and that one moment did not, and should not, define her as a person.

I knew she wanted to be reassured that I was happy and doing well. The comments people blogged and e-mailed made her feel awful, and she took them to heart. Online, I argued that the people who had negative things to say had no life. I defended her.

They sat behind their computers judging others when, in reality, I didn't think they were happy with their own lives. It was a form of bullying. People could say whatever they wanted to online without anyone knowing who they were. They could say something hurtful and mean and then go about their day. It infuriated me.

I told her that these people must have never had a true friend and that was sad. We were lucky to have each other, and I still would rather have her as my friend than the use of my legs. People writing hate weren't worth her time or her tears; we talked a lot about that.

From our conversations it became clear she had started to believe what people were writing about her. I told her all the time that she was not stupid, evil, or reckless, as everyone implied, and that she didn't deserve her guilt. People actually wrote that she deserved to be miserable. These were comments on blogs and following online media stories. I told her that the people judging her had most likely done something in their lives that could have caused someone injury, but they were lucky to have sidestepped that fate. People didn't realize how easily a spinal cord injury could occur.

Helping her heal became my mission: Her happiness would be the final piece to mine. I wasn't healed until she was.

From there it just poured out. She told me she had major anxiety attacks and that she watched that night play out in her head, frame by frame. Every single day. She told me she was worried that someday I'd hate her, but I think she knew deep down I wouldn't. She apologized for bringing it up because I think it had actually sunk in that I wanted her to be happy. I think she knew I was okay with it all, but she felt despair inside. It wasn't that she didn't believe me. She did. It was like a waterfall of emotion that she'd carried inside for six months, and the word *prank* broke her internal dam. It just shattered her, and she was reeling.

I couldn't believe what I was hearing. I was worried about her. I was even more worried than I had been before. I knew it was really bad, and I knew I would have to help her. The irony was that, honestly, I *was* happy. I was happy to be alive, grateful to be in love, and thankful that I had so many great friends and family members. Sure, I was scared, and some days rather terrified, but I was happy inside. I knew she wasn't. I knew I had to focus on putting aside my own issues, and I decided to take on hers.

One day I said to her, "I have physical pain. You have emotional pain. But they are so different. Don't carry this sadness forever. I don't intend to."

I decided during that conversation that I would be her pillar of strength forever, and I told her that. I felt like our friendship was so strong that our shared experience would get us through this together. I told her she could always talk to me. I became her spine. I channeled optimism for her. I wanted to save her. I knew I would be fine, but I didn't know if she ever would be.

CHAPTER 22

Wedding Plans

THE FEBRUARY AFTER I RETURNED HOME, CHRIS AND I DECIDED to go ahead and pick a wedding day. We chose July 22, 2011. Part of our decision to lock in the date was due to 1-800-Registry kindly coming forward, offering to give us our dream wedding. They'd seen the story on *Headline News* and called for my information. I knew it would be wonderful but very different than the wedding originally planned. I was nervous about being wheeled down the aisle, not walking, and I was pretty terrified that our first dance wouldn't be what I'd always dreamt it should be. But I knew who my bridesmaids would be, and that gave me a lot of comfort.

Along with all the media attention came a couple of generous and interesting offers. In addition to 1-800-Registry, *Today* offered to pay for my wedding and cover it live. And *George to the Rescue*'s remodel of my home had made our bedroom a real oasis. It was suddenly green, with hardwood floors, and it had a roll-in shower and a low sink and granite counter I could roll under. The decor was beautiful, and they installed an elevator that saved me. The wedding was shaping up to be just as spectacular.

All of the girls of course knew they'd be in my wedding, even Britney, who hadn't been a part of the original party. The good fortune of having the wedding sponsored meant I could include Britney, which I'd told her the night of my bachelorette party I wanted to do but couldn't since we had nothing coordinating for her to wear. I was thrilled to have a second chance to include her. She had become such a good friend to me, and we had confided in each other a lot during my recovery. Our friendship had become so deep. Plus, the accident had made her part of the group. I wanted her to stand with the rest of the girls when I said my vows.

Originally, I was to have someone other than Britney standing up there with me: my friend Sandra. She hadn't been able to make it to the bachelorette party, and that surprisingly had some heavy implications for our friendship. It all resulted in a terrible friendship-ending e-mail exchange. We had gone to college together and were really close, especially in senior year. I used to think of her as my Pirate-in-crime. After college she moved to Raleigh, and we drifted apart a bit. I guess when you grow up you start to become more aware of differences that in college you wouldn't have noticed. Sandra and I discovered we had political differences. It wasn't a huge thing, but we weren't on the same page and we wound up not seeing each other as much as we once did.

Sandra had a birthday party one night and I decided to leave early, and she got kind of pissed off about it. A silent tension existed between us, and so the wedding came around and she didn't attend my bachelorette party. She was visiting her cousin, who was going off to war the next day. It was understandable so I was okay with her absence, obviously.

By this point I'd actually been wishing Britney could be in the wedding, but I'd already ordered the dresses for the bridesmaids, and I couldn't find one to match for her. I even checked eBay. I couldn't ask for the dress back from Sandra, and I couldn't ask for everyone to buy new dresses.

Then the accident happened. I was growing so close to these other girls, but Sandra and I were getting further apart. She lived fifteen minutes away and never really came to visit, and for whatever reason, that upset me deeply. Believe me, I appreciated that people had busy lives, but a friend is a friend and I had an expectation she'd show up when I needed her. She said I should have invited her, that she wouldn't just appear, but it felt a little weird to ask someone to visit me at home. Mostly, people called and asked if they could stop by. They asked how they could help or if I needed something specific picked up. Sandra kept saying, "I'm going to stop by," but never ever did. At one point I said, "Stop saying it if you're not coming." In her defense, we had already drifted apart. I thought that maybe she didn't feel comfortable coming over. She supported me in the way she knew how. She did visit the hospital a couple of times and, after the accident, she threw a small fundraiser for me and I was grateful for both gestures. I just needed more friendship from her and she from me. There were some lonely days when I first returned home, and I needed a lot of support.

The tension broke, and it sounds so immature but we had a Facebook fight, and she said something that threw me completely off guard. She said that she was frustrated in the hospital that she had to wait so long to see me. She meant the night I broke my neck. My own family had to wait to see me; the girls who were actually there, who had to experience that traumatic event, hadn't even seen me, and she was frustrated and had the nerve to tell me that. In retrospect, I think our argument got out of hand and we both reacted poorly. This happens to a lot of friendships. Our relationship just wasn't strong enough to override the hurtful words we had both said.

Once we both cooled a bit, I wondered if it was simply too weird for her to see me in my new environment. The hospital actually might have been more comfortable in some ways. It wasn't a new reality, just a stopover. It was possibly my first realization that people who had known me once as an able-bodied person might feel uncomfortable around me. Maybe she also held some guilt for fighting with me or not attending the party that night, which is crazy. But the strangest part is that I think she saw the five of us together, who were all at the pool, and she felt left out of that bond. It would have been hard to break through it; we had a shared experience. The stronger my friendship became with the girls by the pool, the more difficult it was to maintain the flimsier ones. The girls by the pool became the gold standard, and not just in how they treated me, but in how they treated each other. It was really unbelievable and admirable to have witnessed the growth of our relationship.

Then on the other hand I had Sandra actually saying things in an e-mail like, "You don't know how singled out I felt, to be the one who wasn't there." Maybe I would have felt left out in the same situation, but she should have been happy that she wasn't part of that event. I've learned that I really don't know how other people feel or how they should react. It has all been a good lesson in empathy. You just don't really know what people are actually thinking inside. Maybe the four who were there filled up so much room in a positive way that my friendship with Sandra was one of the casualties of this accident.

It turned out she did feel guilty, which she later revealed. She wrote, "I don't wish I was at that party. I did at first because I thought, if I was there could I have done something to prevent it? I felt guilty for not being there . . . but I felt like I should have been there. I thought, if I had been there what would have been different?" In her final note to me, she wrote something that startled me. She said, "You have no idea what it feels like to be the one person who wasn't there to witness what happened, who you don't even speak to anymore. I'm sure you've called all the girls who were there, but you haven't called me at all." It shook me up and we never spoke again after that. I wasn't sure if the bond with the other girls had grown so large that maybe it blocked up space for other people to enter that circle. Either way, Sandra sadly wasn't included in the new wedding plans.

I called the girls individually to make sure the date was okay with them and explained that, since it was being paid for, we'd get new dresses, too. That, of course, was very exciting to them. They didn't love the original dresses.

As we made plans to wed, I also scheduled surgery to have what's called a suprapubic catheter put in—a permanent tube that was to be inserted into my bladder and attached to a bag strapped to my leg. I was told it would be convenient because I could open it up myself and go to the bathroom by myself. There was still a bag attached and it would be a 24/7, like a ball and chain, but I was excited at the forward momentum of everything.

New dresses aside, everyone was ecstatic that we were finally going to have the wedding, but there was one concern among all of us. We'd navigated the murky waters of the press, careful to keep our promise not to reveal exactly what had happened that day. We had done a good job in protection mode as a team. But a televised wedding meant more coverage and more discussion. It meant all of our faces would be on TV. Of course, one girl in particular felt panicked at this prospect.

Today and 1-800-Registry decided to team up in a joint effort, and it was incredible that they'd both donate so much, but as we got into the planning, we learned that *Today* could air only a five-minute ceremony. Sadly, I realized that wasn't for me. That was to be the most exciting part of the wedding, and I wanted to cherish it, not rush it for five minutes start to finish. I'd waited so long for it. I hated to miss the opportunity, but I would have rather had the wedding in the backyard than compromise the ceremony like that, despite how grateful I was for the show's generosity. For me, the most important part was our vows. I didn't want to be rushed for commercial break. A meaningful ceremony was far more important than being on television.

It also alleviated another concern—no faces live on TV. I told the girls of my decision and heard a collective sigh of relief.

I was sincerely appreciative of everything *Today* had done for my cause. They were the most wonderful people. And I was eternally grateful and happy that 1-800-Registry was still on board even if *Today* wasn't part of the wedding anymore. So 1-800-Registry handled everything, and I was able to choose all of the details.

The planning began. Again.

CHAPTER 23

One Year Later

ON THE FIRST ANNIVERSARY OF MY ACCIDENT, I WAS ON THE WAY back from an Abilities Expo in New Jersey. I had met the people at Colours Wheelchair, who had sponsored me and agreed to donate a really amazing wheelchair to me. I had attended the event to meet Rick Hayden, who ran the company and whom everyone called Big Daddy. I was going to choose the details for my chair. He was nice and hilarious and was the one who had asked me to be part of Team Colours originally, months earlier. I selected a blinged-out chair with spinners and suspension and was fitted, because anyone with an injury like mine needs a customized chair. They're quite expensive, and I was honored to receive such a lovely gift. Also, I had hoped it would give me confidence because it was so pretty, with Aztec designs and bright blue colors, but the experience with the other girls I met on that trip tapped into some insecurities I hadn't realized existed yet.

I was feeling a little shyer than usual meeting these beautiful Colours Girls. They were all paraplegics, and it was hard being the only quad among the little group. I remember feeling self-conscious, because I needed so much more help than all of them. I was fascinated by what they were able to do: They could easily transfer in and out of their chairs; they could lean over and just grab something off of the ground; they'd go to the bathroom together like any other group of girls. Their bodies didn't even look paralyzed. They just looked like able-bodied people sitting down. They had no quad pooch, which I had developed; my belly protruded due to inactivity, and it made me look pregnant. And obviously their hands weren't balled up like mine were.

What made me most self-conscious was that their hair and makeup were perfect. Mine used to always be perfect. I knew that if I could do my own hair, I could look just as nice. I knew how to do my hair better than anyone, obviously, because it was my hair. So while it was a great experience, it was also just a reminder of how disabled I really was. We all went out to dinner the last night, and I felt so *not* cute. My mom was there and she tried hard to help me get through it, but that night I was probably more sensitive than usual, and even though my hair did look nice, I felt insecure. These girls all looked hot. I wanted the use of my hands so I could look just as hot.

We came back from Jersey, and I was relieved that I was going to be able to see some of my friends. My mom brought back a giant cannoli from a New York–style deli, and we celebrated her birthday. Admittedly, there was a bit of sadness and negative energy in the room as we celebrated her birthday, but as I had hoped, the new chair eventually gave me a lot of confidence.

Looking back at the year that had passed, I knew a lot had changed and taken its toll on all of us, but through it all, I was certain my love for my family and friends had grown. Chris and I became more aware of what we had as well. We'd always been affectionate, but in the wake of the accident, after a year of being in it together as a team, we'd learned to be so grateful for each other and our love. After we returned home from rehab, Chris got into the habit of hugging me as soon as he walked in the door, a gesture I greatly anticipated each afternoon. We'd mindlessly done it before, but after the accident we did it with intent. At night, as we lay in bed, he would say, "I love you, sweetheart" and then I would rub his back gently until he started snoring. Each morning, he made my day by saying, "Good morning, beautiful." We never left each other without a kiss and an "I love you" exchange. None of that routine was lip service either, and I knew in my heart it would always be our way. The year that brought us so much tragedy had also enriched our lives. We never let one day pass without our special moments. We'd become painfully aware of how quickly and drastically life could change. No one knew what the next day would bring, so neither of us wasted time not loving one another fully or taking our love for granted.

Chris and I reaffirmed our love for each other. I was amazed by how many people found this difficult to believe. It made me think that many people, those who questioned whether he would stay with me, just don't know love. Love clearly wasn't as common as I thought it was. It was hard for me to imagine that just because of a physical problem, a perfect relationship between two people who loved each other wouldn't work. I only wished more people had that love for each other and could understand what we had. If you asked someone who has lost a spouse to cancer or some other terrible disease if they'd take their deceased loved one back if they were in a wheelchair, they'd say yes without question.

I never set out looking for our love to be tested, but I was glad—and not remotely surprised—that it survived. I never expected my strength in general would be tested or that I'd be forced to push the limits of that strength, but I was given no choice. I was always a careful girl, and I thought I was doing everything right. I was safe, or I tried to be. I really didn't have to think about strength before, whether I was or I wasn't strong. If you'd asked me as a twenty-four-year-old, "Hey, how would you manage being a quadriplegic?" I'd have said, "I wouldn't want to know. I don't think I'd handle it well." You just don't know until you need to know.

CHAPTER 24

The Rehearsal

JULY FINALLY ARRIVED, AND THE THURSDAY BEFORE MY WEDDING was the most hectic day. Mom and I were rushing around, and I was kind of stressed out. We had a lot to accomplish before we left town for the rehearsal and the wedding. I had to worry about my hair and my tan. I had had an opportunity to have hair extensions put on for free, but because of timing, I missed the window. So I was freaking out a bit, like any other bride, because I wanted my hair to be perfect. I had the actual hair extensions but no one to attach them. I found one guy who said he could do it for three hundred dollars, but that was way out of my price range. I didn't expect it to be so challenging. Finally, after many frantic calls, I found someone who was available and who gave me a really great price.

For me, the wedding was not about the flowers, the food, or any of that. It came down to two things: One, I needed to look great. Before I got hurt I used to say all the time that I wanted to look good. I wanted it to be the same after the accident. I wanted to look as good as any other bride, knowing I would be upset if I didn't. It wasn't about having the perfect wedding day, but looking good still mattered. I wanted to look good enough that no one saw the wheelchair, that all anyone would say was, "What a beautiful bride." Two, I needed Chris to be there. That was the bottom line.

Part of looking great meant that the tan and hair were integral parts of that equation. I had solved the hair problem, but the challenge of the tan was full of additional obstacles. I used to get spray tans all the time where you stand up and get sprayed. But that was when I was able-bodied. Luckily, I found a woman who would come to my home since we'd have to adjust the methodology a bit to get it done.

"Normally, we set up a tent so your home doesn't get spray tanned, too," she explained. "You'd stand up and I'd spray you."

I laughed. "Obviously, I can't stand up in the tent. We'll have to figure something else out."

She was so nice and not weirded out at all, which made me happy.

"I've seen a ton of people naked," she said. "We'll figure something out."

We brainstormed a bit and decided to do it in my bedroom on the bed, with me lying down. It was a production and it took about an hour, because we had to spray and dry, spray and dry. I was flipped around, and at one point my mom had to hold up my legs one at a time so we could spray those.

In the middle of it all, Chris came home and had no idea that I was getting a spray, and no idea that there was a random person at my house in our room. He came in the bedroom and opened the door. He made the funniest face and said, "All right," and closed the door and went downstairs.

After all of that, the tan was overly dark and I had to do a little scrubbing to lighten it up.

We had an intimate bridal shower at the wedding site, which was so nice. The wedding was being held on a dairy farm in Pittsboro, North Carolina, with a hotel on the grounds called the Fearrington House and community called Fearrington Village. There were cows in the field behind us while we got married, so you can imagine the setting. It was really country, which was what I wanted.

My shower was originally planned for the day after the bachelorette party. So I'd never had one. I wore a flowing maxi dress that was very casual. With all my extensions in, my hair was long and straight, very hippielike. The shower was in a beautiful room, set up on a terrace with windows all the way around. It was an open and elegant space with a Victorian look to the furniture. It had a big floral carpet with a large wooden table in the middle that held all the food. My mom brought a cupcake holder, and we had these hilarious drinking cups with noses drawn on the side of them. They were just plastic cups, but when you took a drink, it looked like your nose; some had mustaches, some had nose rings, and some were really big. We played a few games, such as "Who Knows the Bride Better?" and we all laughed when my mom guessed my eye color incorrectly. My eyes are hazel, and my mom wrote green. Lauren won the game. Britney was late and could come only for the rehearsal, but Samantha and Carly drove up together and made it to the lunch.

Coincidentally, all the girls matched. Lauren and Samantha were both wearing coral dresses, and Carly wore a tan dress with a coral flower in her hair, and a fifth bridesmaid I had added—a woman named Mayra who worked with Chris and had become friends with us—wore floral, too. By the time the rehearsal took place, it was a typical hot and steamy July evening.

During the rehearsal we all had a good laugh because Chris and I practiced our kiss, which I hadn't really expected to be any kind of problem, since we'd kissed a million times before. It turned out to be the funniest part of the evening. I had no core muscles, so I couldn't lean forward and kiss him or I'd fall right out of my chair. Carly wound up having to sort of block the chair so it wouldn't roll backward at that very important moment. At the same time Chris had to hold my wrist to pull me toward him. He had to hold on firmly so I wouldn't fall. I fell over a couple of times until we got the right balance. Chris caught me. Next we had to practice putting on the rings because I didn't have finger function. He obviously put a ring on me, but I wanted to put his ring on him, too. We thought about it for a long time, trying to ensure it was meaningful. We finally came up with the solution to put his ring at the tip of my finger, then he'd connect his fingertip to mine and I'd slide it on—like a fake push from me, and he did the rest. Chris's uncle Ron came up with that one. He was the minister performing the ceremony the next day.

After all the laughs and the rehearsal, I said goodnight to Chris. He kissed me and said, "I love you."

I said, "I love you, too."

He said, "I can't wait to marry you. I'll see you tomorrow."

I remember thinking, *Wow, this is finally happening.* We were ready to be married. We had waited so long, and it was so exciting. It was fun getting his friends and my friends together and having this wonderful time that we'd never been able to have. I was thrilled that it was the last time I was going to see Chris before I could finally call him my husband.

That night, Carly, Samantha, and I all stayed together in one room. It was like a slumber party, and we had so much fun. Every time we were sort of drifting off to sleep, someone said something, like when you're fourteen and having a sleepover with friends and someone keeps talking. It was the greatest night.

CHAPTER 25

The Perfect Wedding

WHEN I WOKE UP ON JULY 22, I WAS NOT JITTERY AT ALL, BUT I had happy anxiety. It was my day, with my girls by my side. I was excited about my hair and my dress, and I was overjoyed that they were all there for me and were all going to be part of it. I had so many happy thoughts. We had people who had donated their time to fix our hair and makeup. One of the makeup artists was actually the wife of a local radio celebrity named Mike Morse. Chris listened to his show every morning and was a big fan. Our wedding planner knew him, and Mike offered to MC the wedding at the last minute. We'd already lined up a band and DJ, and now we'd also have Mike as our MC. It was a huge surprise for Chris. We didn't tell him that Mike would be MCing our wedding and that his wife, Lindsay, did our makeup. She is highly requested around our area for makeup and he's often requested for parties, so we felt like celebrities.

I have two *really* vivid memories of my group of girls. One, of course, was the night of the accident—that's seared in all of our heads. But the other, the bookend of my thoughts of them, was on my wedding day in the early morning. Those girls were as important to that day as Chris.

We were all getting ready together in this really pretty little room. Lauren, Carly, Britney, Samantha, and I were all having our makeup and hair done, just like we had before we headed out dancing the night of the bachelorette party. We needed three hairstylists to keep things moving.

I had to get into my dress, and we knew ahead of time that might prove to be a challenge. I wanted to keep my wedding dress—the one I had bought originally, before the accident. It was definitely one of those "This is the dress" moments that I had with it, so changing it was not even remotely an option. Even if 1-800-Registry wanted to buy me the fanciest dress on the planet, I wouldn't have been able to accept it. I had fallen in love with mine. My mom really wanted to buy my dress, and she had worked so hard to make the payments on it. We couldn't afford it all at once, and she had made the final payment right before the wedding. I was in love with the dress, and it was so meaningful to me.

So 1-800-Registry paid for the seamstress to fix my original dress. She had to take it in a bit, but it required a much larger alteration. The back had a corset that laced down and then exploded into a train. The train had to be removed, because I certainly couldn't sit on top of that crazy pile of fabric. It would have filled my chair. We laughed really hard when we tried to put it on a couple of months before the wedding, before the alteration. We pulled it over my head, but you couldn't see me. It wouldn't go down over my head, so it looked like a person with no head and long legs. Everyone laughed as I sat there covered in dress, and someone said, "Nope, nope, this won't work." Which of course made us all laugh harder.

Essentially, after much thought, we decided to have the dress sliced open up the back, so that when you unlaced it in the back, it literally folded open. I had to do this so I could get into it. There was simply no other way for me to put it on. We tried. It was hard enough to put on a wedding dress while standing up with help. Putting it over my head with me sitting wasn't an option. So that day, we had to lay it down on the bed, spread it out, and open it up, almost like a wrap you would make a sandwich with. After much deliberation I had to lie facedown on the bed and get my boobs lined up, and then someone had to lace me up while I was there facedown. It was pretty hysterical, I have to say. They had to keep moving me around and shifting body parts to line things up. Obviously, I was totally over being naked in front of people—you lose that shyness after an injury like mine.

We were all laughing and giggling, and the moment felt perfect. It was eight in the morning. I didn't normally drink coffee, but I was tired so I had a cup and it actually tasted really good. It was probably because I loaded it up with cream and sugar. I remember at one point looking around and feeling like this was the start of something better, the beginning of a new chapter. I felt like some healing would occur because the wedding was no longer something that had been taken away. It was given back to me, and I was overwhelmed with happiness. It was given back to my friends, too, especially the one who had pushed me and suffered so much for that act. I was so grateful they were all there. These girls were more than just bridesmaids to me. In fact, I had not one but four best friends who were all like sisters. My wedding wouldn't have been my wedding without them. But my favorite part about that morning as we got ready was that no one mentioned the accident, the wheelchair, or the reason we were glued together for life. I am sure no one even thought about it. It was just a happy day. A beautiful, happy day.

It was so hot that day—102 degrees. Everyone was laughingly complaining about the heat. Out of the blue Carly began to put baby powder between her thighs.

Of course ridiculous laughter erupted.

"What the heck are you doing?" I asked.

"Well, I don't want my thighs sticking together from all the sweat!"

We shared ten minutes of real laughter. Everyone was throwing the bottle of powder back and forth, and it was hilarious. They all looked so dignified and dainty all done up, but they were still acting like their goofy selves, and it felt so normal and good. I didn't sweat anymore because of my injury—most C-level injuries don't sweat because the part of the nervous system that controls that function no longer works. I was also always freezing, so the heat didn't bother me at all. But we were laughing hysterically about the baby powder. All of them were hiking up their dresses and trying to delicately put powder on their thighs without getting it on the dresses. They'd gotten these new beautiful, flowing J. Crew dresses in turquoise, which went really well with the country setting and the sunflowers they would be carrying. They loved the new dresses, too.

Every moment of the wedding was amazing. I had always dreamed of a country wedding—something very Southern. I just thought I would like something rustic. I had really wanted to get married in a setting with a barn. I had Googled "North Carolina barn" and "North Carolina barn wedding," and one of the results that came up was this perfect place. I originally thought it was more of a casual setting, but it turned out to be extremely fancy. On the grounds of this dairy farm was a beautiful five-star hotel, and it had appeared in many magazines. The barn was not just a barn; it was like a reception hall, quite elegant with chandeliers

© MARTHA MANNING PHOTOGRAPHY

everywhere. I didn't expect all that, but of course when I saw it, I thought, *Oh, definitely.*

I could see the ceremony beginning outside. I watched each bridesmaid make her way down to where she would start her walk. I think they were more nervous than I was because they were being videotaped, but not by any TV cameras, just our own cameras. Plus, I was a center-stage kind of person. I didn't mind being in front of big crowds, but the bridesmaids were worried about tripping down the aisle. At least I no longer had to worry about stumbling down the aisle in heels.

I know it must have been hard for my friend who pushed me, because it was only one year after the accident, but that night by the pool was completely off limits. This was not a day to reflect on the incident by the pool, and everyone knew that. I was grateful for that unspoken silence. We were all looking forward to my wedding day, even though she hadn't healed. Still, I took great pleasure in looking down the aisle, knowing she was happy and she seemed to be getting caught up in the moment with us all, having a good time. I'm sure it was hard for her, but it would have been sad if she hadn't been there, sad for me. I think she knew that. Plus, I knew that seeing me marry the love of my life would give her a little bit of inner peace.

It all felt real when I watched my bridesmaids walking down the aisle, and I thought to myself, *Wow! They're going and then it is my turn!* As my dad pushed me in my wheelchair, I was looking at the crowd to see who was there, instead of looking at Chris, and then suddenly I was at the front beside him and my dad kissed me on the cheek.

It felt to me (and my mother said this, too) that the wedding day wasn't only the day I'd committed to Chris, but it was my finish line. It marked the end of the ordeal, the end of the interruption from the accident. It felt like things had come full circle.

The setting was perfect. The only rough part was that Chris and I had to sit a little farther apart than I would have liked. My chair and the chair he sat in facing me couldn't really fit any closer together. But we held onto each other and it was all okay. Better than okay.

Our vows were incredibly special. I remember them vividly. We said the same thing to one another. I said, "I, Rachelle, take you, Chris, to be no other than yourself. Loving what I know of you and trusting what I do not yet know, with faith in your love for me, through all of our years, and in all that life may bring us. I promise to be ever open to you and above all to do everything in my power to permit you to become the person you are yet to be. I give you my love." I was smiling as I said that, though I thought I was going to cry. I was just so happy to be there that I didn't stumble over the words at all. We each repeated them after his uncle said them for us, a few words at a time. We kissed after that, and then, in Jewish tradition, Chris stomped on a glass. Carly was holding my bouquet. I turned to go back down the aisle without taking it. She said, "Rachelle, don't forget this." I turned and looked, and really loudly I said, "Oh, crap." Everyone laughed.

After the vows we had a special moment to ourselves. We went in this little room, and even though everyone wanted to congratulate us, we took five minutes to be alone together. There was no conversation. Chris just hugged me tightly and kissed me. And we looked at each other with this amazing shared excitement.

What I cherished most about my wedding day was my first dance as Chris's wife. The entire day felt like a movie in my head being played second by second, but one beautiful moment, my favorite, was the first dance. Chris and the guys wore dark grey striped tuxedos with turquoise ties to match the girls' dresses. Chris wore white on white—white tie, white shirt—and a sunflower boutonniere. I took a moment to absorb how he looked as we were getting ready to dance. We hadn't practiced it before our wedding day, and I was nervous even though I figured it couldn't be that difficult. Who would have ever thought my dance would be done from a chair and that still it would be the most memorable, heartwarming part of my day? We danced to "Won't Let Go" by Rascal Flatts. The chorus fit perfectly; it's all about never letting go of the person you love and being there no matter what. I had actually switched the song to something

© MARTHA MANNING PHOTOGRAPHY

by Corey Smith, but the DJ hadn't made that change, so Rascal Flatts came on. It was funny and yet so perfect. I'm glad it got chosen for us like that.

There wasn't a dry eye in the house. We did twirls all over the floor and everyone thought it was rehearsed, but really it just came naturally and was totally spontaneous. It wasn't being able to stand up that I missed during that dance, but I wished I could have used my hands so that I was able to hold Chris's hand during our dance. He held my hands, but I would have loved to hold on in return. I wished we could have been able to embrace one another. As someone who loved dancing, I never thought I'd be wheeling around the dance floor with my new husband. But it was still an amazing moment that I will never forget.

My maid of honor read something at my reception that had meaning to a lot of people. It was a quote from Bruce Lee: "Love is a friendship caught on fire. In the beginning a flame, very pretty, often hot and fierce, but still only light and flickering. As love grows older, our hearts mature and our love becomes as coals, deep-burning and unquenchable."

I know people find this hard to believe, but there was never a moment where I felt sad about being in the chair that day. I really, truly didn't. I had a dream wedding. I had had a dream bachelorette party before the accident, too. The wedding wasn't about walking. It was about love. It was about the man I loved and my family and my friends being there for us, together. Walking wasn't a requirement for celebrating. I don't think anyone else had any sad feelings, either. In fact, it might have been more meaningful to everyone. It might have been more significant and a reason to celebrate because I'd survived. It was just a bride and a groom and a great ending to a terrible ordeal. It was as sweet as everyone else's wedding. I had all the trimmings and fun and an awesome husband—more than everything I'd dreamed of.

After that, at the reception, a Southern band played and we cut the cake. The photographer and videographer zoomed in on the knife. We were trying to cut our Funfetti cake, my favorite, with the knife upside down. I blamed Chris. I had no grip, so he was holding it. We included all the fun traditions like throwing my garter, which was an ECU Pirates garter purchased for the original wedding, and tossing my bouquet, which I did as Beyoncé's "Single Ladies" played in the background. My brother was dating a really cool girl named Becca, whom he had met at one of my rugby tournaments. She was also a quad due to a birth defect. He flew her up from Florida for the wedding. She caught my bouquet. A guy from my rugby team, Ronnie, also a quad, caught the garter. So that was pretty cool and kind of fitting.

We gave everyone blue bracelets for spinal cord awareness and we made a donation to the Miami Project, whose goal is to cure paralysis, in the names of everyone who had been invited to the wedding.

BraunAbility had loaned me a van while I planned my wedding, but I never imagined that they'd actually give me one. At the end of my wedding reception, everyone lined up outside to throw yellow rose petals and blow bubbles as Chris and I made our exit. We rolled down the middle of a long row with everyone on either side. We turned a bit as there was sort of a bend in the crowd, and there it was: this big van covered in a white tarp with a bow. They pulled it off to reveal a sporty Toyota Sienna that didn't look like a soccer mom van. I was in love. Later, a local company called Van Products installed hand controls, which didn't require hand function, but just the strength in my arms to maneuver, and a transfer chair. The driver's chair moved back and turned with the press of a button, so that I could transfer in from my wheelchair.

Chris and I did not consummate our marriage that night. Everything had been romantic and sweet, but we were too tired. I was playing with my little nephew after the wedding. We were trying to throw a football in the room, and I was lying on the bed. He wrapped my hand around the ball for me. He was really good with the injury. He asked if we could watch a movie, which made Chris realize it would be a long night, so Chris and his best man went to get ice cream. I thought they were coming right back, but they were gone for a long time because Chris thought I was hanging with my family. It was funny. He finally returned, and we ate some leftover food from the wedding. We were exhausted by that point, so instead of having some passionate night as man and wife, we just crashed.

Chris was like Prince Charming sometimes. When he was feeling romantic, he'd hold my face and rub my cheek and look into my eyes, and he often said the sweetest and most genuine things. On this night, as we were falling asleep after the most wonderful day, he turned to me and said, "Rachelle, I could never live without you. I'm so excited we are starting our life together. You were so beautiful today."

I said, "Thank you." We kissed. "I loved our dance together."

"Everything was perfect. The dance was perfect," he said. "The whole wedding."

"I wouldn't change a thing about the day," I said. "Nothing went wrong, either," I said laughingly.

He grew serious again, looked me straight in the eyes, and said, "I wouldn't want to spend the rest of my life with any other person. Just you. Forever."

I always felt we were two halves of one whole, but that night, it was official. I was his other half and he mine—and it was forever. We'd beaten all of the odds and skeptics because we knew love. We had true love. Our souls had connected.

CHAPTER 26

The Finish Line

Something unexpected happened following my wedding that I heard about only afterward. My girls—who wouldn't have met had it not been for me, and who wouldn't have bonded as strongly if they had not had a shared experience by the pool that night—went out after the reception and had the greatest time, the four of them and their dates, plus Chris's best man and Mayra.

I was told later they had been worried initially about the one friend who had suffered, but after spending time with her that day, they could see that she was really happy to be a part of it all. That night, after Chris and I left, they talked about their new perspective on life, and how much they cherished it. They said the wedding ceremony itself was closure for all of us, so they danced and partied their butts off afterward and had the best time ever. It was their night, too, I think. In fact, some of them weren't even going to stick around that night, but this crazy party erupted among them. I actually felt a little sad that I missed it, but I was glad that they found peace in their own way, too, together. Apparently, they all just let loose and had a blast for the first time together since the bachelorette party.

I think this marked a nice ending for my troubled friend. I wanted her to have a good time, and it sounds like she did. It was a really big deal for her that day. It was important to her that I got married and had that milestone. It was probably the real start to her healing—to see me happy and to know that love had not been taken away from me, that the one thing I wanted had only been postponed, not stolen completely. It was as important to her for me to say "I do" as it was for me. It was good for her to have these girls around her. They all protected each other, and that came out collectively on the dance floor as they burned off one year of steam.

CHAPTER 27

Paradise

WE LEFT IN THE MORNING AND HAD OUR FIRST NIGHT IN VEGAS. It was so much fun gambling for the first time, but we wound up losing, of course. We got tickets to see *The Lion King*, courtesy of 1-800-Registry. I'd never seen anything like it before—it was amazing. We stayed at the Mirage Hotel. I thought the lights and the strip were the coolest thing ever.

After the night in Vegas, we headed off to Fiji, which had always been my dream destination. I never thought in my wildest dreams I'd be able to travel there. We flew in and had to take a helicopter ride to our destination, which was called Tokoriki Island. It was breathtaking. We had a large bungalow at the Tokoriki Island Resort with a huge bed and white linens, and we could open the windows and the back door and it felt like we were outside even when we were inside. It was just a ceiling, and the walls were basically open. The shower was outdoors and had blue tile.

Everything was blue. The water was blue, crystal blue as far as you could see. There was an infinity pool that Chris would float in; we could sort of see the edge of it, but then it would blend in with the ocean. There were palm trees everywhere. It was gorgeous.

Of course all of the food was amazing, but my favorite dish was at breakfast. Pancakes covered in powdered sugar—so good I couldn't get enough. We ate every meal on tables outside, looking at the ocean. It was truly paradise. At dinner the waiters would play music. Once, our waiter came around to us and asked if we wanted a love song or an upbeat song. I said both. They started playing Jason Mraz's "I'm Yours." I couldn't help but sing along.

Chris learned to scuba dive while we were there. That was something I used to do and always wanted him to learn. They allowed me to go on the boat with him even though it was rough. I just sat there and held on tight. The workers were so nice, all native Fijians from the local village. They carried me on and off the boat. We took two trips over to the local village, which was our favorite part of the trip. It wasn't exactly wheelchair accessible, so Chris had to lean my chair back and wheelie me over a lot of the terrain. It seemed like none of the kids on the island had ever seen a wheelchair. I let them touch it and spin the spinners. The inside piece actually spins, kind of like a pimped-out car you might see, except I spin these manually. They loved it.

Some other kids approached me on the trip and wanted to know what had happened to me, so our guide, Vili, told them in their native language. He knew my story, as we had become good friends while we were on the island.

Chris did a lot to help on that trip, even going so far as to put waves in my hair with a wave-making iron I had brought along. It turned out he was very particular about wanting to make my hair look good. He'd talk me through it, saying, "Hold still. Wait a minute. Almost done." It was pretty darn funny. One day, we plugged the iron in and it totally fried. We just stared at it in disbelief. We had a good laugh about that.

While we were away, absorbed in luxury and sunshine, the media had apparently gone absolutely crazy because the wedding stirred up the story again. We did get some time on the Internet there, so we read all these crazy stories and the comments. I was amazed the world had taken such interest. We were scheduled to fly to New York when we returned from Fiji for appearances on *Today*, HLN, MSNBC, and *Inside Edition*. It was exciting and exhausting all at once.

Of course, when we first arrived in Fiji, we were very tired. That kind of travel was something I'd certainly never experienced. Plus I was jet-lagged. But after we caught up on our sleep and overcame the exhaustion of our wedding and the trip, we finally consummated our marriage. It was really wonderful. I wrapped my arms around him and he kissed my neck, and it was passionate and loving. A moment I'll never forget.

CHAPTER 28

My New Reality

WHEN WE RETURNED FROM FIJI, WITH THE WEDDING BEHIND US, it was time to start moving forward and figuring out what I would do with my time. The wedding and my healing had taken up a lot of my efforts, and the media appearances surrounding it all had been a whirlwind.

I started to find that my days weren't very interesting. I wanted to work, of course, but the nerve pain made me an unreliable employee, sometimes taking over my body for hours in the morning and often into the afternoon. Still, in the months that followed our wedding, I began to grow increasingly aware that the fast-paced, media-infused life I'd been leading wasn't real, and with the wedding planned and done, well, suddenly, everything stopped. That's when I was confronted with really understanding my injury and learning to handle it. I knew I had to do something to fill my days and figure out what my next steps in life would be.

That meant my friends became that much more important to me. Those girls by the pool were suddenly everything. I had Chris to look forward to at the end of each day, and I loved seeing him and eating dinner with him, but I found myself relying more and more on them. In fact, there had been a dramatic shift: I had been their strength, especially for one of them, but now I needed them badly to help me figure it all out.

I found that all of them helped. Samantha suddenly had such a calming way with words and situations; that was her gift to me. Britney was always there to talk and kept me company, as some days stretched on and felt endless. Lauren was always that friend who responded to texts in the middle of the night, no matter how much time had passed, and Carly was the one who provided me with the most random laugh over the most absurd thing, always right when I needed it.

That support helped me make some big decisions. I decided to return to doing what I loved before I was hurt: coaching the Wake Shakers, the seniors cheerleading team. They participate in local and state senior games that lead to the Senior Olympics, with all different events, including sports but also acting, singing, and cheerleading. Right after college, I was working with kids in an afterschool program, and these seniors were using the back room of the same facility. I had to set it up for them before I left, and I overheard them talking about needing a coach.

I jumped into their conversation and said, "I'm here anyway, so if you want help, I'm available."

They took me on. I felt bad because I'd taught them all of their cheers, but then I got hurt. I was supposed to add dance lessons, but I wasn't able to. They had to scramble to find someone to help right after the accident. Still, I was able to return, and they were excited to have me. It was really nice to know they missed me, and they said that they'd never let me go again.

Since we had a specialized van, I needed to learn to use it. So that became another project for after the wedding. At first it was really helpful for my mother to get me around in it. A small car was challenging. The first time my mom drove me in my van, I was strapped in, but somehow I shifted and tilted and eventually fell back flat. We laughed our heads off. I called moments like that "quad moments."

Eventually, I had to take steps to learn to drive myself, so in July 2012 I decided to get started. I needed to get used to just getting into the van. The way the van was set up made it possible for me to drive alone, but it was a physical undertaking at the same time. I had to use all of my strength to push my wheelchair up the ramp and into the van, and then getting into the driver's seat meant using every available muscle in my arms, as well as a slide board. I didn't have the strength to lift myself, so I learned to slide myself. I had to get used to steering once I was inside, too—and it also required more arm than hand strength. To turn the wheel I kept my right hand wedged between triangulated pins surrounding my wrist, and to apply brakes or gas I kept my left hand on the hand controls. It was completely different than anything I'd ever done. Just sitting there the first time I got in was really scary, and I knew I'd be afraid on the open road. It was nerve-wracking. Add to all of this that I had never driven anything larger than a Honda Accord before the accident, so driving a van felt like driving a spaceship. I knew it was going to be a challenge.

Like everyone else, before I really even got going, I had to struggle my way through the DMV. It was a huge ordeal, and I had to argue with them to obtain my permit. I needed a permit so I could learn to drive with an occupational therapist first, but they repeatedly told me a road test was in order. I made arrangements to meet with the therapist, but I never took that road test.

I couldn't. My car would not be fully adapted until after I trained with the occupational therapist. The therapist evaluated me to see what I needed. I finally made the DMV workers understand.

There was another hurdle, though. I trained with the occupational therapist in her car and it took some getting used to. I had two hours of fiddling around, and then this woman made me drive on the busiest interstate in my region. It was trial by fire, but I pulled it off. After just four hours of one-on-one training, I took and passed a driving test.

I realized quickly that I liked the independence. I would take an occasional trip to T.J.Maxx just to go look at clothes and be girly, but it always took a lot out of me energy-wise. One afternoon, I took a trip to the mall, and while there I rolled by a kid who was clearly intrigued by my chair. I heard him say something to his mom about it.

I stopped and went back and said, "Wanna see something cool?"

He said yes.

I spun my spinners for him, and his eyes lit up.

He asked, "Can I try?"

I said yes, of course, and he loved it. He didn't want to stop. He finally did and I started to roll away.

He yelled, "Wait."

I did and he came up and gave me a huge hug and a kiss on the cheek. It was a great moment, and I hope it changed that kid's view of people in wheelchairs or of anyone who might be different. I loved that his mom hadn't pulled him away. I had started to notice that some parents yanked their kids away from me so quickly. I tried that afternoon to teach at least one kid that we are all the same. I hope, in some small way, I helped to eliminate the ignorance so often instilled.

So I took small trips on occasion, but driving to one place took four transfers, which I learned was exhausting. It meant I had better *really* want to go somewhere badly to make the trip. Nevertheless, because being so dependent on others was frustrating, getting my driver's license helped somewhat. It allowed me to more easily visit my girls and some days to just take a ride to get out of the house.

When I first started learning, there was a huge debate between my driving trainer and me. She insisted I should get rid of my manual chair and get into a power chair. I had been adamant about staying in a manual, so it was sort of frustrating and took away from the excitement of the situation. Yes, it's easier to get up the ramp and to roll yourself in and drive from your chair. But there are basic freedoms taken away when you choose a power chair. I'd never be able to ride in my friends' cars, because they couldn't transport the chair, and Chris wouldn't be able to pop me up and down stairs. I wouldn't be able to simply be wheeled out onto the beach. So even though transferring to the driver's seat is more difficult and time consuming in a manual chair, I was never afraid of hard work. I could push, so I wanted to push.

Driving made me feel normal. Cleaning my house did, too, and so after we were married I made an effort to be a typical wife and to provide my husband with a nice home to return to at the end of each workday. Unlike some people, I hated cooking, and that never changed. But I found that after the wedding, and as the media attention died down, I liked the peacefulness of cleaning, so I tried more and more to do things like laundry by myself.

CHAPTER 29

Let It Be

THREE WORDS SUMMED UP MY LIFE BEFORE THE ACCIDENT: LET IT Be. My dad used to sing to me when I was little. He didn't sing lullabies; he sang songs by the Beatles. I knew "Hey Jude" and "Imagine" by the time I was five years old. One of the songs I loved most as a kid was "Let It Be." The song had an early impact on my life, and the lyrics were words to live by for all of us—my family, friends, and me. When my friend Carly and I sang in the hospital, we sang that song often. Of course, when I was out of rehab, "Let It Be" lingered in my mind, well beyond the white-board it was written on that had made it our group mantra. It grew to be my mantra and our way of coping. It was a term that defined how we came to realize our bond without actually saying much about what had happened, and it was critically important to me and to the group. It gave us all strength.

I was being interviewed on the news about the accident, and I mentioned that I wanted to get a tattoo on my neck. Shortly after, I received a phone call from this really cool guy at the Blue Flame Tattoo shop. He'd seen the story and he said he wanted to give me a tattoo for free. I was excited but also a little bit afraid.

But with such a nice offer, I couldn't say no. I had to go through with it. I made the appointment.

I called my brother to share the news. He already had so many tattoos and he'd done so much to help me out that I wanted him there to share the experience with me. The day of, we grabbed my mother and headed out to the shop. I decided to have it done on the back of my neck. I'd thought about that area for a tattoo before the accident, but not for any reason as meaningful as this one.

Breaking your neck at the C6 level affects movement and feeling from the chest down, as well as triceps and finger function. The neck doesn't actually experience paralysis until you reach the C1 or C2 level, which are the very first bones at the top of your spine. Many people think, "Oh, you broke your neck, so you are paralyzed from the neck down," but that's not the case. *Quadriplegic* just means impairment in four limbs, not necessarily full paralysis. So I felt pain in my neck, which I guess made the tattoo more significant and ironic at the same time.

Just saying *pain* doesn't really describe it. It hurt. The tattoo was applied right where the bone was on the neck, so I think that was why it hurt as badly as it did. Still, hair pulled back, leaning forward with my neck exposed, we got down to business. It was excruciating. I don't know how many words in, I yelled, "Stop! I can't take the pain anymore."

My brother said, "You're barely halfway finished; you can't stop now."

I thought about it for a while, then took a deep breath and said, "Okay, let's keep going." In case I might forget just how horrifically painful it was, my brother snapped a ton of pictures of my miserable face wincing from the needling.

Another problem also slowed things down. Whenever my body experienced pain or infection, it often responded with muscle contractions or spasms. This was the case during the tattooing. We had to take a lot of little breaks to deal with my body's reaction.

But at the end of it all, I was set to remember, for life, those three special words that have been my guiding light. I had *Let It Be* and a peace sign inked onto the back of my neck in the exact spot of my injury. Chris and I have talked a lot about getting a couple's tattoo to ink our bond, but I wanted this one first. I wanted a permanent reminder that I had made peace with my situation, that it was what it was, and that, simply, the only way to get through life is to just let it all be. Having it in ink on my neck gave me secret strength. Knowing it was there powered me, and those words both literally and figuratively became a part of me.

CHAPTER 30

Buckets of Love

Chris and I had agreed we would spend the rest of our lives celebrating our love and never letting an opportunity to make a memory together pass us by. We had gone to visit his family in Ohio over Christmas break, and while we were lying in bed, we starting talking about how we enjoyed celebrating love and doing things for one another. We of course already made a big deal of Hanukkah, Christmas, Valentine's Day, and our anniversary, but between it all, we had a five-month gap with nothing to celebrate. We decided as we were lying there to make our own day, for only us to enjoy. Later that day, we hopped on the computer and started searching holidays for that time period in the gap, looking for something random and funny that we could celebrate. There's a day for everything, but when we saw My Bucket Got a Hole in It Day, we knew it was ours, and it was timed perfectly in May. It was random and goofy, but we marked our calendars, both excited to celebrate.

When the first one came around that next year, I bought Chris a subscription to *Bassmaster Magazine*. His dream was always to have a bass-fishing boat. So I opened a savings account and put $100 into it because, hey, you can dream and you have to start somewhere. He had waited until the last minute to buy me something and got a little panicked by his decision. He had to call my mother on his way home for suggestions about the perfect gift. He settled on a pretty engraved key chain that said "Chris & Rachelle Driven by Love" on the front and "My Bucket Got a Hole in It Day" on the back. He wanted me to have a special key chain as I perfected my driving skills. Ironically, Chris's dad had a bucket with an actual hole in it. We created a tradition in which we'd put our gifts in it for the exchange. We take a picture with that bucket every year.

Maybe I did take for granted the simple, obvious things before the accident. I hated going for runs, for example. I hated going to the gym and preferred to relax after work. I know those are normal feelings for many people, but if I had my old life back right now and the ability to walk, there are so many things that I would do. . . . I'd go for runs, rock climb, travel more, hike, and see some of the big mountains. I'd do all these things and make sure that I didn't let a week go by where I didn't do something new or awesome with my legs, something that required physical ability.

Our Bucket Day grew to become really important to me. I needed to cherish all the little things in life, because some of them were fleeting. Looking back, maybe I would have simply done more when I could walk. I worked at the senior center and as a lifeguard, and that was my life. I am not saying it wasn't a good life. I had a fun job—I loved working with seniors and I loved lifeguarding. I just didn't do enough. I didn't appreciate the ability to dance then, for example. It's unlikely we would have come up with another celebratory day for our love if I hadn't learned how important the appreciation of these things was. People need to appreciate every day. I even looked back and appreciated the ability I once had to go to the bathroom on my own. I started speaking to groups, and that was always my message: Take advantage of running or dancing or even the simplest things while you can.

CHAPTER 31

What If

FOR A LONG TIME, THE ACCIDENT AND THE WHAT-IFS WERE ALWAYS part of the conversation with the girls. Not overtly, but they were the elephant in the room. One night, as we approached the two-year anniversary of the accident, we were all hanging out at Samantha's house in the living room and something shifted. It was a mini-reunion almost, not planned as such, but we just happened to be together. We were gossiping and catching up, which was our favorite thing to do.

This particular night, with all of us hanging out, the accident didn't loom. The sadness wasn't masked with laughter. It felt gone. I don't know how else to explain that. It's as though it didn't matter to us, as a group. Individually, sure, I am certain we were all dealing with it, but as a group we'd been liberated from it somehow, and this casual, uneventful night was only about fun and laughs and friendship.

One of the girls was really nervous because she had to have her wisdom teeth removed.

"I'm freaking out about it," she said as we all sat around chatting.

"You'll be fine. It's just the dentist," someone else said.

"I'm scared," she kept saying.

I said, "Geez, I broke my neck. You can get to the dentist."

We all erupted in laughter. It was different laughter. It was like something significant had changed in a good way, especially for the friend who had so playfully and innocently pushed me. She laughed, too. Finally. We all did. It wasn't somber anymore. The accident had become fair game. It didn't own any of us. It was one of those markers, you know, those moments where it's all different, and although the pain still existed, it didn't fill up a room anymore. We could genuinely laugh. I don't think I would have made that joke a year earlier. She was just too sensitive about it then. Everyone was. It was raw, and the guilt and pain consumed them all. But I remember the shift so vividly. We could all feel it and see it and hear it. We were girlfriends again. We'd all come out of this okay.

That night, it became clear as we talked that we all felt guilt to a certain degree. It had come up over time, little by little, but it took us nearly two years to really address and solidify our feelings. We all felt it in different ways. My friend who helped me get out of the pool that night told me late in my stay at the hospital that she felt badly about the fact that maybe she injured me more on the scene by listening to me and pulling me out of the pool, instead of stabilizing me. I assured her that I really felt like the damage had been done when I hit the bottom. Another friend felt that maybe she should have caught me or done something— that she could have prevented the fall if she could have reached out and grabbed me. To me, that was so illogical and her guilt so unnecessary.

One friend told me she watched it all happen in slow motion and, looking back, believed that she could have prevented it.

Instead, she called 911. I felt guilt, too, about my split decision to dive instead of allowing myself to fall feet first. I even felt guilty that I was afraid to go into the water. *What if I had just walked into the pool at the steps, instead of hesitating or talking about it being too cold to jump in?* My friend who pushed me watched that scene in her head like a movie, frame by frame, and every time, she played the "what if" game and was then overwhelmed by anxiety. We felt guilt for all the times before as kids and adults that we had played around by a pool. I'd done it. They'd done it. Thinking of all the times before made us cringe, and nothing even happened then.

If only one little thing had been different or we'd been standing in different places. They all wondered if it could have been one of them who got pushed instead of me. I wondered what would have happened if *I* had pushed someone that night, which of course could have been the case. I am sure they all would have rather not been there given what happened, but no one ever actually said that to me.

For all of us, it was a loop in our heads, and we were finally at a point where we could share our feelings on the matter, which to me meant the healing perhaps had really begun.

What if I didn't push her?

What if I didn't complain about the cold and had just gone in on my own?

What if I hadn't made it downstairs because I was still inside?

What if I had been able to catch her?

What if I had not made us go swimming in the first place?

What if we'd stayed out longer?

What if we'd gotten drunk and were too drunk to go swimming?

What if it had been the next night instead?

Airing our feelings like that opened a door for us all. A month or so later, a bunch of us got together for Samantha's birthday and we had the most amazing time, in part because it was fun and we were all together, but in part because no one said a word about the accident again, something that had been slowly happening with increasing frequency. It was becoming a pattern. There wasn't really any kind of deep conversation at all, just pure fun like we used to have back in the day.

The night began at Samantha's house. Before we left Chris stood behind me and helped me look like I was standing up with my girls, and we took an old-fashioned group picture like the night of my bachelorette party. Chris was the designated driver, so it was his job to chauffeur us to the club. My van has a nice amount of space, and along the top it has an outline of blue light. We blasted the music, and for one night it was more like a pimped-out party van instead of a wheelchair van. We were all dressed up, too, and we went to a rooftop club.

I felt a real change that night: It didn't feel unique or special or out of the ordinary. It just felt completely normal. Can you imagine striving for normal? Not spectacular or anything insane. I was just so relieved we were back to 100 percent regular, raw fun. We'd had so many nights together where the sadness filled the space. They made the rest of the talking feel forced. But not this night. This night, it was just plain real and normal. And I cherish that night when nothing else was with us but friendship and love. It took a long time to reach that moment, but I think once we did, a lot changed forever. We couldn't roll backward in any way because the healing had begun.

CHAPTER 32

Keeping My Head in the Game

AFTER THE ACCIDENT I HAD TO WORK REALLY HARD TO TACKLE the mental aspect of my life—which grew to be the more challenging part. Life sometimes felt kind of lonely, though I've always hated the negativity that stems from that word. Since the accident I hadn't figured out how to connect with my old friends, other than my core group of girls. I missed college, but I hadn't figured out a way to connect with many of my college friends, mostly because it had become clear that going out was a challenge for me. Crowds were difficult to navigate and I always got so cold.

So I figured I'd bring the crowds to me. I decided I would hold a party at my house, for the first time since my accident. It was going to be a college party, though no one was actually in college anymore. I put together a list of people, ordered a keg, and set a date. I was really excited that most of the girls could make it, that we could be together again. It almost happened, but at the last minute Lauren said she couldn't come.

Samantha and Carly came early to help set up, although we were laughing that there wasn't much to put out besides the beer. We bought a keg, but college parties don't have real food, so this one didn't either. They'd driven down together and were staying the night. Once the essentials were in place, they had to quickly do their hair.

Britney came, too, with her new husband. They'd gone out to watch the ECU game for a bit at a restaurant and then stopped by. She was the person I attacked with joy when ECU claimed its first basketball championship in the CIT. The Pirates won on a three-point shot at the buzzer, no less. The entire crowd went crazy.

I invited a bunch of people—the guy friends I had in college, people I hadn't seen in forever, and people who lived in the area. When I was in college, I had the perfect party house. It was up on stilts because it was close to a river, so I could have people over and everyone would just hang out underneath the house. I didn't have to let anyone inside, so no mess. We had parties all the time, and I really missed that. And, to be honest, I had so many good friends from back then that I hadn't seen since before I got hurt, and I wanted to see them.

Before the accident it was so much easier to go out, so it was nice to have people come to me and be in my environment.

It was really hard to make new friends, being injured and no longer being around people as often. In college it was so easy, because you had neighbors and you had dorm mates. People my age found friends through work or some group they were in, but I couldn't work. So the way adults typically made friends was difficult for me.

I had friends who were nice and we were Facebook friends, but I think we would have been really close if I were able-bodied. It would have been easier for me to just drop by and visit them. I wasn't in a position to grab lunch at a restaurant or meet up with girlfriends, which they probably did more on a whim. So it was hard. I was growing more independent, but I hadn't developed enough confidence yet to drive on my own and just go meet up with someone. I guess that's why my friends from before the accident were so valuable to me.

About twenty of my tight friends came to this party, and they were the ones who had been in my life for a long time. Sometimes I felt a little awkward around new people. I had become less confident because I knew people were sometimes uncomfortable with the chair. I'd met some cool people, but I got a little self-conscious about things like not being able to shake someone's hand. I didn't have a grip, and shaking hands was just what people did. I was sure it was noticeable and put people off sometimes. I didn't blame people for being uncomfortable. When people meet a quadriplegic for the first time and don't have a history with them, I think it's really hard for them to see past the chair, and then it's hard for me to get past the point where they're not awkward. So it was nice, if only for one night, to feel like I was living back in the old ECU days, with crowds and a keg and a bunch of friends around me.

Carly and Samantha came into my room in their pajamas after everyone had left, at two in the morning, and we sat up talking until five. Chris just snored away in the bed; he can sleep through anything. We began talking about how we really wanted to see more of each other, saying that we should try to get together at least once a month. I needed them in my life. They brought me joy. The past was the past, and college was awesome, but these girls had kept my head screwed on straight and had become my present.

I had to come to terms with not walking, but that took a lot of mental exercise, too. I had accepted the overall situation, but I struggled a lot with body image issues, just like most women do. Mine were the same as most people's, with some differences, like the quad pooch. I tried on tighter shirts that I used to wear, and all I could see was my belly. Since I taught aerobics before, I had a pretty good body, but my core muscles deteriorated, and I started to feel really sad when I looked in a mirror.

I actually grew jealous of lower-level injuries as well. Many paraplegics have function in their core, so they get to keep their abs. Of course their arms and hands have full function, too. I met so many paras during the first year of my injury who were so down on life because of their situation, and all I could think was, *Come on! Your hands work! You were independent within a year of your injury.*

Two girls I met right after my injury were paraplegics after each was in a car accident. They had been dancers before being injured but continued to participate in wheelchair dancing. I wanted nothing more than to be able to do that. To move my arms like I used to and to gracefully use my hands. They would do spins in their chairs while popping wheelies. It was actually pretty awesome what they could do. As someone who had danced regularly, it was hard to watch, as beautiful as it was. They gave me advice once.

"Once a dancer, always a dancer," one of them said when we were talking about it. This was true in my heart but not my reality. Sure, I was able to go on the dance floor and jam a little to the beat, but I will never do any choreographed dancing. I'm not talking about messing around. I missed dancing so much. It was my favorite thing to do, and I wished it hadn't been taken away from me. It was the one activity I wanted back.

I was always the dancer in my relationship with Chris. I took ballroom dancing before the accident, and I loved Latin and salsa. Chris would occasionally agree to dance with me, but generally he didn't really dance. He had two left feet, in fact. I always used to have to try to drag him out on the dance floor and say, "Come dance with me," and I teased him by saying, "If you're not going to, I'll dance with someone else." I never did. Even though he was a bad dancer, I loved dancing with him. Every once in a while when I was out with my girls, there would be a guy on the dance floor who really knew how to Latin dance, and I would dance with him. I never wanted to turn down something fun like that, although I would have rather danced poorly with Chris than well with a stranger any day.

There were people who had it worse—some higher-level injuries than me who would give anything to have the arm strength that I still had. Some quadriplegics would give anything just to breathe on their own. High-level quads want to be low-level quads. Low-level quads want to be paras. And high-level paras want to be low-level paras. I realized independence was the most significant measure, and that every hardship is relative in this world.

I had to work on not getting frustrated by how people behaved in front of me. I noticed some were extremely uncomfortable, but others were okay. I realized educating people was my job, and I started to work on landing more and more speaking engagements to help enlighten people.

I was thrilled that from the second I was injured, my friends treated me like just another one of the girls. That was always important. Some people, mostly when I met them for the first time, would bend down to get to eye level to speak to me. It wasn't insulting if someone couldn't hear me, but otherwise it sometimes seemed demeaning. Strangers thought that since I was in the chair, they needed to treat me like a child. Some patted me on the head and others who were my age called me sweetheart or honey, which I didn't think they would have done if I were ablebodied. I hated being treated like a dog or a kid.

My friends never scrambled to help me with things I could do myself, even when they saw I was having a hard time. They waited to be asked, which was cool. When you help someone without asking them, it takes away the only independence they have left. If I could push myself across the sidewalk, that's something I needed to do. Picking things up off of the ground, driving, and putting on my shirt were now all things that I didn't take for granted. I didn't want people taking the few things I could do for myself away from me. I had lost enough.

CHAPTER 33

Marriage

BRITNEY GOT MARRIED ON MARCH 22, 2013, AND I WAS REALLY excited to go to her wedding. When I got engaged, I'd known Britney for maybe eight months. We were more "going out friends" than anything else at the time, but I knew I liked her a lot. I was glad she'd come into my life. This whole new level of our friendship grew in such an unexpected way.

She'd go for a run and just swing by my house and sit on the couch for a talk. It was easy for us to spend time together, and we would go downtown and have lots of laughs. And more than the other girls, we had face-to-face time, for talking about everything, and that was really nice. It still is.

I was with Britney before her wedding. We were getting ready together.

"Are you having fun?" I asked.

"Yeah, for sure. It's so cool to have all of these people here for us," she said.

I agreed.

"Do you remember the night before your bachelorette party?" she asked.

I didn't really. I remember a lot of stuff, but of course the night itself had been more memorable.

"Not really," I said.

"We stayed up really late. You don't remember?"

"No," I said.

"We talked about ghosts and spirits. We were up all night."

I loved that she had this crazy memory of that time. I loved that she remembered some really fun stuff that had nothing to do with the accident. Ghosts and spirits had been the topic of conversation, not anything else about my party.

With Britney wed, that meant she joined Lauren and me in commiserating about the ups and downs of being married. Despite the hugeness of our love story, Chris and I have had some tense moments, like any other couple.

Lauren had gotten married four weeks before my accident. Our birthdays were so close together, and then we were almost married around the same time, too. We also had similar relationships. Their relationship was easy, like ours. I connected with her on that level. I was supposed to be born on her birthday, she on mine. I was glad I was paralyzed *after* her wedding because it would have ruined her day. She was the person who had always been in my life, like family, since I was two. I don't even remember meeting her; she was just always there.

One night, Chris and I made the three-hour drive up to visit Lauren and her husband; we all went to hang out at a sports bar near their house in Charlotte. Lauren told me that night that she'd cried at work, in front of her boss, the Monday after the accident. We also talked about how the accident had really tested my strength.

I remember sitting there during our dinner and thinking that I was actually glad the injury hadn't happened to anyone else. I handled it. I'm a patient person. I don't mean this offensively, but Chris is a stresser. I'm not sure he would have been as easy about having someone take care of him as I have been. He overanalyzes things, too. I thought about that as we sat there, how his traits, or anyone else's, might have impacted their ability to deal with this situation. I'm calmer, I think.

Chris and I never really argued. Neither of us were fighters. But he misdirected his frustration sometimes, and I knew that. We had disagreements, of course, every couple does, but we weren't the type of people to raise our voices. We never yelled at each other. Some people wondered if he controlled himself because of the injury. It was not that. He didn't cut me any slack. There was a time when we butted heads over what I was actually doing for myself and not doing for myself. He wanted me to be as independent as possible. It was the kind of head-butting that only came out if he'd had a stressful day at work. In year two of my injury, when I was better able to handle the nerve pain but had also figured out how to do a lot for myself, I'd get lazy. He'd come home and we'd be watching TV, and I'd say, "Can you get me a glass of water?" And some days he'd get it, but on some days, he would say, "You are able to get it yourself." He was pushing me. He'd say, "You want to be independent. I want you to live as full a life as you can." He was right. It took me longer to get a glass of water, but I could get my own water. Absolutely.

When my body was on fire and I was in pain, it was hard. It was hard to be motivated when I felt that way. There were days when I was struggling and he'd come at me wrong. But it was a good period in time to learn, about each other and about myself.

Sometimes I actually was so drained and felt so guilty about the situation that I cried. At the end of each day during this little rough patch, we'd sort it out. We never went to bed angry.

Communication helped us survive all of this. Neither of us ever held back on sharing our feelings with each other. We understood that both of our feelings were valid and that everything we felt was always okay. I believed nothing got fixed if you avoided talking about it. We resolved a lot, and I felt stronger for it. You don't know a lot about yourself until you are tested.

CHAPTER 34

The Big Shift

It took two and a half years, but the day finally arrived: My friend and I talked about anything but the accident. In a group setting there were so many laughs, and in private we had them, too. But there was a long stretch of time during the media blitz when not one phone call or online chat or get-together transpired without her saying she was sorry that this had happened. Think about that: I saw or spoke to her hundreds of times, and every single time she was sorry, and every time I swore to her it was okay. And then, suddenly, we turned this amazing corner, and we were just girlfriends again. Even after the shift, of course I knew the accident would always be there, but I finally felt like she looked at me and didn't just see the accident, but *me* again. We had finally recovered something that we used to have.

Someone once asked me if I'd rather bear her burden or mine. I gave that a lot of thought over the years. I think she suffered far more than I ever did in the beginning. The accident, fooling around by the pool—it changed her as a person. She eventually gained her footing and came back down to earth, but before that it was something that was constantly in her head. She could never escape her guilt. For someone in my situation, there were support groups, resources, and sports. I had so many people to turn to for help to guide me through my life. There wasn't exactly an "I accidentally hurt my friend" support group. So when I thought of that question, I knew it was a lonely feeling for her, realizing that there might be no one out there who could relate to how she felt. I guess the only difference was that it was also easier for her to hide from her situation and demons than it was for me. When she was able to shut herself off from anything that reminded her of the accident, she operated fine.

Physically, she was still able to do things, whereas physical limitations were always going to be a part of my life. She probably didn't pass a day without thinking about the accident. But I hoped it didn't bleed into every aspect of her life like it did mine. At least it would be possible for her to have normal days, and I would never have another "normal" day, not my old normal anyway. I never resented her for that, even though I knew it was hard for her to be around me, even though I had to be her support group and we both knew I was the only one who could help ease her pain. Unfortunately, it was a double-edged sword, because she had to see me and remember why I was in my wheelchair. Every day was like reopening a wound. That's why when our friendship turned a corner, I was ecstatic. It was no longer all about that night. The impact evened out, but we suffered differently, and we accepted that finally.

I think about how the roles could have been reversed and wonder how I'd handle her situation, because honestly, it could have been any one of us pushed in the pool that night. It was so innocent and playful and random. But when I imagine suffering through my pain or her pain, I honestly think that in the end, I would choose my own situation—maybe because I know only what these shoes feel like.

It's not new or scary for her or me anymore. I think that makes it easier for her. One time I was sitting on the bed, and she could see I was hurting a bit and uncomfortable. I tried never to let her see this side of things. But this time I was dizzy, so there was no hiding it. I could hardly move. I could see the look on her face, and I said, "I know this looks bad, but it's really not."

We erupted into laughter. It actually *was* bad—I was feeling awful and struggling. But by just saying it, I guess it finally became okay to laugh about it with her. Humor had been one of the main things that had helped us endure this ordeal. Then we returned to talking about girl stuff. And the elephant in the room just disappeared.

Neither of us thinks it will ever be gone from our lives completely; that's naive. But just to have days when we're together and it's not part of the equation, or stuck in the back of either of our heads, is a huge step forward. Even actually being able to talk about that night at all, without it being scary or sad, is a relief. Things are just more logical now.

I don't want to suggest that her healing didn't come from inside, because it did. It had to. You can't get past this kind of horrific event without your own strength, but I feel proud that I played a part in saving her and protecting her. I know what revealing her identity would do to her, and I want to protect her forever. Her secret is forever. She shouldn't even have to hide it as a secret. She did nothing wrong. But people can be cruel, so we have all decided that no one else needs to know. This unbreakable friendship, it's a real thing between us all.

There's no doubt that we all survived because we worked as a team, worked together to stay strong and hold each other up.

We all had moments of weakness, sure. But we had to weave our way through the jungle—the night, the hospital, the media, *Oprah*, the cruel comments. Beating those experiences was a team effort.

In the early days after the accident, I could feel her pain without her saying a word. I began to notice a shift in her aura finally. She just looked happier, and I noticed it without her telling me. She'd shed a skin almost. I don't think she'll ever forgive herself completely, and if she could go back, she'd change it all in a heartbeat. At least she learned and finally believed she didn't do anything wrong; it was an accident, and we're able to laugh again. The laughter has replaced the angst.

Something else happened, too—something really significant with her, and it had to do with the press. People were saying that I had shared my financial struggles with the public to gain sympathy and get donations. Of course, that was ridiculous. For starters, it was part of my story. It was part of the discussion. Being in need of different medical attentions meant I was very familiar with the shortcomings of healthcare, and those shortcomings are usually about money. I was grateful for all that people had done—remodeling my house, giving me the equipment and training I needed to drive again—but accepting these wonderful things didn't make me a bad person. Neither did enjoying a dream wedding and honeymoon; I was happy with the ceremony I had originally planned and would have had it in my backyard if need be. Plus, I had no idea any of this would happen. How could I? It happened quickly, and I didn't seek out the attention at all. People were just kindhearted and helped. I would have done the same if the tables were turned and I was able.

But all of that aside, I'm not the only person suffering or living with this financial problem. I shared my shortcomings in relation to healthcare and insurance to shine a spotlight on a critical issue. I was fighting the fight and hoped my efforts and the attention I received helped others, too. My accident and recovery made me no more special than anyone else with a disability.

Shortly before the three-year anniversary of my accident, I was doing a catch-up session with the online discussion site Reddit in a section called "Ask Me Anything." I received more than a thousand questions. *Today* did a follow-up online in response, titling the post "Bride Stays Positive in Spite of Financial Struggles." People of course piled on and judged me based on that. There were so many mean comments. I called my friend who had once been haunted by these kinds of words. I couldn't hide how upset I was, and I told her what had happened.

"You've done so many positive things from this injury. Ignore the haters!" she said. She was giving me the same advice I'd given her so many times before. I had slipped. I was allowing myself to be emotionally affected by the ignorance of these people, all for my honesty. It made me so angry. It didn't make me feel bad about myself, but I felt bad for society. People were judging me for no reason. She stood up for me. She supported me. The tables had turned. I had felt comfortable enough to share, and she had become strong enough to help. It was a powerful moment.

CHAPTER 35

Being Heard

I STILL HAD ONE THING TO CONQUER THAT I HADN'T SINCE THE accident: I wanted to sing again in front of people. In my efforts to remain really busy and meet new people whenever I could, and to not let this wheelchair ever get in the way, I worked hard to find new things to do. I loved my wheelchair rugby team, and I had always wanted to try something crazy, like skydiving, but sometimes I checked out the website Meetup.com to find activities in the area that might be fun for just a night.

Since I loved singing so much—it was always my passion; I loved entertaining people—I was immediately struck when I saw a karaoke night for twenty- to thirty-year-olds listed on the Meetup website. I was excited, but I was also really scared. I used to belt it out all the time before the accident, and Carly and I had done lots of singing in rehab—but I hadn't really tried to sing much after that. Especially not in front of other people. I'd met some cool people through this site, so I decided I would sing and try something bold.

I was just going to wing it. Tom was there and Chris and Mike, too (another friend, not cousin Mike). I was wearing a burgundy mini-dress and brown leather boots. The event was at a pretty cool place in downtown Raleigh, right by NC State, a rival of ECU, and I think the drama school was there; they were belting out amazing tunes that night.

I had to coax myself a little in my head. I kept thinking, *You've been singing all of your life. You feel pretty right now, which is important. You're dressed nicely. You can do it. You can do it.* I kept saying this in my head as I watched other people get up to sing.

When I was little, I was always performing. My friends and I would make up skits and shows, and we'd sing for our families all the time. I loved it. When I was in high school, every year I did the talent show. I always chose a Shania Twain song. One of them was "Honey, I'm Home." I thought back to high school and remembered that people really got into that country music. I decided as I flipped through the book to channel high school and stick with a crowd-pleaser. So I did.

Chris helped me get up there and get set up. I wasn't even nervous because I really never got nervous on stage. I was more worried because I knew I lost my breath so easily now, and I could actually get dizzy from exerting myself. So that was one concern for sure. But I had practiced at home to make sure these new issues wouldn't slow me down. I had speakers in the walls at home and a karaoke system, and I practiced often.

But this came up on a whim and was my actual debut, and as I looked out at the crowd I had this crazy adrenaline kick. I just started singing my heart out. I don't even remember if I thought about it. It just came so naturally and was so much fun. The crowd was totally into it; they sang along and cheered a lot at the end.

I felt really proud that people liked my performance. When I looked back at the video, which we put on YouTube, it actually looked like I was nervous. I had to hold my arm across my stomach and push on it to keep the blood pressure up—it kept me from getting dizzy. So to someone who didn't know better, it looked like I was holding in my butterflies. But I wasn't. It was a really meaningful night for me for sure. It had been on my list of things to do since the accident, and I felt happy to have accomplished it.

CHAPTER 36

The Positive

I THINK WHAT BOTH SURPRISED AND INSPIRED ME THE MOST SINCE my accident was the attention my story received. I had no idea when I was released from the hospital that it would reach anyone. Then, suddenly, I was in the news. What I appreciated most as I watched was that my determination, my character, and my personality somehow got through to people, and that really gave me confidence; it made me feel good. I felt like I did beat this injury, turned something negative into something positive by reaching out and impacting people. It was like a light switch went on, and I was forced on a new mission in life determined by circumstance, not fate.

The realization followed my first appearance on *Today*. People donated a lot of money, which was amazing, but they also sent letter after letter to my Facebook inbox and my e-mail. I read and responded to every single one, or at least I tried to. I did it because it made me feel great and I knew people wanted to hear back from me. People wanted to relate to me and wrote things like, "My son had this happen to him," or "I am married to a quadriplegic." They were trying to connect, and I quickly learned I had the strength to help them. I had spent a lot of time dwelling on the hurtful comments, but eventually I found purpose from my accident in the positive comments and the people seeking help.

I realized I could connect with people and let them know they shouldn't just *think* about changing their lives when they read my story, but that they really needed to *live* that change. I knew that, in many instances, my story would air and then I'd be out of sight, out of mind in a sense. But when I heard stories about real changes people had made, that's when I knew I'd made a difference and done something amazing in the years following the accident. It was easy for me to say, of course; I had a constant reminder. I lived in this chair.

So I set out to do what so many had done for me: help a recently injured patient. One in particular was fifty-three when he had a motorcycle accident. (The driver of a van had failed to yield.) I visited him in the hospital often and began giving him and his wife advice. It was so hard to look in their eyes and see the sheer fear and shock when it was all so fresh. But I told them that I was there for them day and night.

I was given a new job following the accident: Fight for the cause I lived, work hard for a cure, raise awareness, and be strong for others. As I sat by this man's bedside for the first time, I knew I had a mission for life.

One night, as the third anniversary of the accident approached, the girls and I had a conversation. We were all sitting on the couch at Samantha's house in our sweatpants. I remember we were playing the board game Apples to Apples, where someone draws a card with an adjective on it while everyone else puts down a card with a noun that they think best represents that adjective. Most people don't play the game realistically but instead put down cards they think will be humorous. It was a silly, mindless game, but fun, and we liked that. I had recently visited my high school to give a speech, so I guess the accident was on my mind.

We had the frankest discussion that night about how they had all changed. Someone said, "It was the worst night of my life." I think I was surprised by how horrified and terrified they all still were when we put it on the table. It will never be forgotten. They all admitted that they think about the accident regularly.

It is a cliché, but we were all made newly aware of life in a very different way. We were so happy-go-lucky before. We never woke up thinking, *Tonight something terrible is going to happen to one of my best friends.* But when it did, everything changed. However, we realized it wasn't all negative; the one good thing that came out of it was gaining a greater appreciation for each other and our lives. Maybe if our friendship overcame my accident, it could overcome anything.

I had two sides to my life. I didn't have the perfect life without problems before the accident. I had ups and downs like anyone. But I did have everything going for me; all of us girls did. We certainly didn't think something like this would get in the way of our lives, and we realized we're not immune to tragedy. Even though something like this happened to me, it doesn't mean it can't happen again to someone in our group in a different way. Realizing that wasn't negative, either. We became healthy and grateful but not immune to reality anymore.

We're mostly grateful for each other.

CHAPTER 37

My Mother's Birthday

On May 23, 2013, my third quadaversary, I received an incredible gift. My friend called me.

I'd grown a little lazy about calling her. I was getting ready to take my mom out for her birthday, when my phone rang.

"Hi," she said.

"Hi, how are you?" I asked.

"I'm okay. I was thinking about you today, obviously."

"How are you feeling today?" I asked.

"Well, I want to tell you that the last three years on this day, I would just sit and look at pictures from the past. I'd feel so sad. I used to have a really hard time with this day. All I could think about was you being in this chair."

"I know," I said. "It's been rough for you. I'm sorry you've had such a hard time."

"Well, I wanted you to know that I can look back at that day now and think of all of the really amazing things you've done from your chair and how many people's lives you've impacted. I just wanted you to know I'm really proud of you."

"I'm proud of you, too," I said.

I knew this moment didn't mean she was all right forever or that she was over what had happened. But it was such a powerful snapshot in time for us both—a considerable step toward healing. It meant to me, at least, that sadness hadn't consumed her, that maybe she was on the way to really feeling better. That's all I'd ever wanted for her and for all of us. I was so happy to talk to her and hear her voice. We'd both grown and we'd both healed, and we did it together.

Everyone always used to ask me what I planned to do on the anniversary of my accident. The first anniversary was tough, there was no denying that. But I had never wanted to see the day the same way many others in my situation might have. I didn't want it to be negative for me. It was a bad day, don't get me wrong. But May 23 was really no different than May 24 or May 25. The days that followed the accident were just as crappy for me as the actual date, so I didn't feel there was a difference on that day.

I think the majority of people attached their anniversary to a specific date, and I was unique in that I'd chosen not to. I decided I would acknowledge it briefly, in my head, but I wasn't going to be sadder on that day. I didn't dwell on that date because I live with this injury every single day.

Some people in chairs who acknowledged their anniversaries grew depressed and anxious. Other people had parties. I thought about doing something to celebrate life. People get killed in accidents every day. I survived. I could have died that day. Instead, I hit at a bad angle, and it wasn't catastrophic. That's a reason to celebrate, and I like celebrations.

I thought of May 22 as the day I'd had my bachelorette party. It's funny because I remembered it as a really awesome bachelorette party, and I think that surprised some people. We had talked about having another bachelorette party before the wedding, but we just didn't. I had had one already, and it was amazing—the best bachelorette party I could have ever asked for. It was the next day, technically, that I was pushed in the pool—May 23—and, oddly, I didn't mix the two up in my head as one event. Maybe for self-preservation or to maintain my sanity, I kept them separate. I remembered the one event as wonderful, and all I'd hoped it would ever be, and the other as not so great, but as something I had triumphed over.

For my friend, because she struggled with pushing me, it was never going to be a day for celebration. I knew that. It had been a sad day for her. Since May 23 was actually my mom's birthday, I wanted it to always be more about that—a special day to celebrate her. I wanted that for my mom, and I didn't want it to be anything negative.

On my third anniversary, I made a wish for the future: I hope someday May 23 will just come and go and the accident, for both of us, will escape our radar for good. I hope, too, that something wonderful happens on this day for my friend, something that eclipses the accident for her forever.

Epilogue

I was submerged again, but this time it was peaceful, even though the force of the waves in the ocean was tossing me around. I couldn't swim because I couldn't move, and yet I felt really calm. I'd been offered a life jacket, but I declined. Having grown up in the ocean, I knew how to hold my breath while I was underwater. With my eyes closed, a few feet under, motionless, I thought back to the accident. It was the floating upward toward the surface that reminded me of that day. I was underwater for what felt to be about the same amount of time—ten seconds. I knew if I had to wait more than five more seconds for someone to grab me, I would have serious problems. I felt confident someone would be there. I had a smile on my face this time. I wasn't remotely afraid. I had that one-second inkling of a thought: *Do they know where I am in this big ocean?* I'd overcome a lot during the past three years, but this experience was a major win for me.

I was underwater, deep in the ocean, because I'd been thrown from my bright green surfboard after riding a wave. I got the opportunity to surf from an organization called Life Rolls On, run by Jesse Billauer. He was a pro surfer, and years ago he went headfirst into a sandbar and broke his neck. He sold me my board and all the equipment to make it adaptive for my injury, such as the straps normally used for kiteboarding. I was able to break it in that day. The Life Rolls On team was all around me, so I felt safe. Before we left the sand, they taught me how to lie on my stomach, propped up on my elbows, which were tucked into a pocket on the board. They showed me how to lean with my body to control the board. Then they helped me get on the board and out into the ocean, where the waves would take over. I had two safety measures offered: I could wear a life jacket and I could have someone ride with me. If I were able-bodied and trying to surf for the first time, I wouldn't have accepted either one. So for my first ride on a surfboard, I ignored my injury and declined both.

Part of the reason I said no to the life jacket was that it was a little more awkward and bulky, but also because of image. It was much less badass. I didn't want to be covered in floating devices. I'm an ocean girl, born and raised. Even this injury wasn't going to put me into a life jacket in my playground. Not a chance. I was going for it. I trusted that the team would come and swoop me up as promised, and in the meantime I'd let the water safeguard me while I held my breath.

There I was, propped up on my new board, with six or seven people around me in the water, on a surfboard for the first time in my life. They had to help me get over the waves. Able-bodied surfers dip their heads under the waves as they make their way out. These guys helped pull me up and over each approaching one. The water splashed in my face and I loved it.

I got out just past the break, and the waves were coming in pretty hard. I was excited but not afraid. The team turned me around, had me facing the shore, and then some of them swam away, back to shore. Just before they pushed me onto a wave, they said, "Okay, ready?" Then one person on either side of me gave me

a push. I tried not to fall off, but I did. I didn't quite have the hang of the board; it was an advanced board, which required some getting used to. I realized my error and figured out the proper way to balance myself once I got back on, by sitting a little higher up on my elbows, with my head up to take a bit of the weight off.

They asked again, "Okay, ready?" I said, "Yup." And they shoved me off and I caught that wave. It was an amazing feeling. I can't remember how long I rode it before getting overturned, but I felt so happy. The water splashed, and I was moving pretty darn fast because I could feel it on my face.

I am determined to overcome the accident. That's a certainty. But I want to be clear that there is an enormous difference between showing positivity and being content with my injury. Just because I work hard and live a full life doesn't mean it's okay with me. I often get concerned that my outlook masks the hardship people like me face all the time and also potentially diminishes any urgency for finding a cure. We can be happy and independent despite our injuries, but this is by no means the life any of us would have chosen for ourselves.

This kind of disability is portrayed very differently than something like cancer, which has more urgency for a cure. I want a cure for this, too, right now. Choosing to be strong and triumphant may make us appear as though we've outsmarted our injury and battled it with a great outlook, but behind closed doors we suffer terribly. Our fight is 24/7 and will be for the rest of our lives. We're a force, too. According to the United Spinal Association, a spinal cord injury (SCI) happens in the United States every forty-one minutes. That adds up to about 12,000 new injuries per year. There are 1.2 million people in the world who currently suffer from an SCI.

I've heard people on a certain reality show that highlights people in wheelchairs say they love life in their wheelchair and they wouldn't go back. While I love what that show does for the community and how it breaks stereotypes, I don't agree with that sentiment. I'd go back if I could. I'd give anything to go back. I hate that my body has turned against me, and that the nerve pain soaks up a lot of my time every day. Mentally, you can be strong to survive an accident; you have to be. You can laugh at all the antics and challenges, and you can have love and support. But at the end of the day, the basic facts of this injury can't be willed away with positive thinking and a great outlook. An injury like this is expensive. To be clear, a newly injured quadriplegic requires between $400,000 and $700,000 in healthcare and treatment. After the initial hospital and rehab work, the follow-up costs are about $100,000. I can't afford this, and I know most people in my position can't. Insurance covers some things, but the 20 percent I have to pay is still beyond my means.

I've always been a fairly liberal-minded person, and I cared about politics even when things didn't affect me directly. I was concerned about human rights and education, but I wasn't really aware of the crisis we face as a nation with regard to healthcare. I'd been young and healthy up until the point of my accident. My parents are young and healthy. Chris and my friends, too. We faced a very expensive crisis after the accident.

The hospital was expensive, and the bills are still stacked up and waiting to be paid. They're not from my original stay so much but from my continuing doctors visits. It's so difficult and overwhelming trying to keep up with everything. Rehab, which I really need, is out of reach. I can't afford to go; just paying the premium on healthcare for us is all we can afford. I was watching the Democratic and Republican national conventions, right around the time I was working on bolstering my Twitter numbers, and I started having conversations with people online, arguing about healthcare. Suddenly my life and my well-being are totally affected by politics.

I'm not eligible for Medicaid. If I were, I'd get a caregiver to help me. That's because I made about $28,000 at my job, so I now earn 60 percent of that through long-term disability. That tiny income combined with Chris's state teaching income would make the monthly deductible around $1,000. We don't have that much money. We can't afford that. I've been fortunate to have had some great organizations pay for stints of care. Walking with Anthony, for example, sent me to this really great place called Project Walk in Carlsbad, California. Medicaid would provide regular rehab, which I can't afford. If the healthcare situation were different in this country, my mom could move back home with my dad and still have her job, and I could get the treatment I need.

Originally, following the accident, I had inpatient rehab at the hospital, which was covered through insurance. After that I received only twenty days of rehab a year. Once those twenty days were up, I didn't get anything additional. I was trying to relearn every aspect of my life, and I had the same coverage as someone who had torn their knee. Rehab costs about $400 an hour until I meet my $3,000 deductible. There's no way I can afford that—not many people can.

Chris teaches middle school, so we're on the state health plan. The cost to cover me alone is $625 per month. That's just for the premium, before the deductible or out-of-pocket expenses. When we were on TV before we got married, the misconception was that we were scheming the system, trying to qualify for Medicaid, and that's why the wedding was on hold. It wasn't a scheme. We were researching our care options; it was sad, of course, that we had to consider our union in terms of how it might affect health coverage.

One of the worst comments I ever read related to the healthcare drama was that I was a "parasite." Someone read my story of love, loyalty, and overcoming adversity and that's what he decided. This person thought that if I married, I wouldn't qualify for Medicaid and it was all part of a big master plan to milk the system.

I was just out of college, without enough work experience to qualify for Social Security Disability Insurance, and the deductible to receive Medicaid would have been much higher than my insurance premium of $625 a month. The irony was that I didn't qualify deductible-free, even as a single woman. I couldn't afford what I would have had to pay. But people were writing nasty comments all over the Internet, saying that I was attempting to abuse the system by putting the wedding on hold. It's as if people assumed that being disqualified from benefits meant that we were perfectly financially capable of going on with our lives without them. But it wasn't like healthcare treatment was some sort of luxury item. Did they think I'd rather be milking the system or able-bodied, working a full-time job, walking, and never needing a doctor? Well, the answer is obvious. And please, who knows any middle school teachers with disabled wives who are getting rich off all that government healthcare?

Six months after breaking my neck, someone even called me "lazy" for not working. Six months! I hadn't even received my fitted wheelchair yet. We were scrambling for some semblance of order, making it up day by day as we went along, but they would see me on TV and think, "She should get to work." I hadn't even figured out how to go to the bathroom, and apparently I was lazy. Before I was injured, I was anything but lazy. I went to college because I wanted a career. I worked fourteen hours a day before the accident and would give anything to do so again. I paid for college. I am still paying for college.

But even more recently, people have uttered horrible comments about the fact that we shouldn't be allowed to have children. We are doing what all parents-to-be do. We're assessing our finances, planning for our child's future, and making sure we can afford to have a baby. We are lining up the support system of our family, which we are grateful to have, and we're going to make our dream come true. The child will be paid for and cared for by us, so it's really no one else's business. Just because I'm in a wheelchair doesn't mean I'm going to be a bad mother. I'm going to be a great mother, just like many women in wheelchairs already are.

The bottom line is that in this country healthcare is a mess. We shouldn't have to think so hard about whether to go to the doctor because we can't afford it. Everyone I have to see is a specialist. I'm a spinal cord injury patient. Every healthcare decision I make is financially motivated.

But what I can do from all of this is defend people who are disabled. I read these comments and respond because I feel like it's my job to stand up to the ignorance and mean-spirited words people write. If they are saying I shouldn't have kids, I'm defending myself on behalf of everyone in my situation because I have the platform to do so. I take it personally and am offended for all of us—the entire society in my situation and the situation with healthcare itself. The ignorance keeps people down. And that really pisses me off.

I don't cry about it, but I become very angry. I wish people would have the guts to say things to my face, so I could more specifically shut them down. But sitting behind a computer, commenting on a thread, is weak. They think I have no voice there, but I do here.

I have developed another voice, too, in all of this, but it's not a good one. It's my own and it's the one that talks to me alone. I know we all judge ourselves. I did even when I was extremely fit, but there's been a lot I have had to accept with this new body of mine, and it's been difficult. I am a new person now. Realizing that has been the ultimate challenge, but I have done it as best as I can. I went from being a lifeguard to being watched over like a child with floaties. I used to teach aerobics and light weightlifting to seniors, and now here I am struggling with two-pound weights, a shadow of the active and athletic girl I once was.

When I was in college, I took a class called inclusive recreation. We had to complete volunteer hours that were relevant to the course, so I chose to assist with the annual adapted sports day at ECU. It was a program that allowed people with all kinds of disabilities to try out different adapted sports and activities. I vividly remember trying out wheelchair tennis. I couldn't wait until it was my turn to get into the wheelchair and hit some balls with a wheelchair user. I don't think many people can say that they've done that kind of class and then ended up a quad.

I've almost taken on a new identity. I used to define myself by that active part of my life, and suddenly it has all disappeared. My grace and ability to dance dissolved in the water. I am like a rag doll moving to music—no more hip-hop classes, no more ballroom dancing lessons. My hands are balled up, and my legs have atrophied.

It has been difficult to accept a deteriorated appearance, too, not just deteriorated function. I didn't expect so much atrophy. It's happened to not only the muscles in my legs, but also the muscles in my chest—and that means my boobs. I've gone from having a solid B-cup to buying bras in the kids' section. My feet swell up like balloons, too. My hair used to fall out in chunks and sometimes I had to wear wigs. I have to hide a lot with leggings and tunics and boots. A lot of sexiness was taken away, but I work on making sexy a state of mind. I work with what I have, and I try to make myself feel good about things. Sometimes just a little eyeliner and lip gloss change my day.

I can't say I love this new body because I'd be lying. That's a happy universe that I have not reached, and in reality I may never get there. I will say that I have made a huge effort to define my love for myself based on what's on the inside. I think once you start really loving who you are, your confidence and positive vibes will be apparent to those around you. And you know what's really sexy? Confidence. I was kind of a sexpot before my injury, so it has really been about getting my sexy back and reclaiming that confidence that I believe allows me to show my inner vixen again. That's not specific to women who are injured. It's something women in general should remember.

That's why I want to tell people who complain about superficial things to cut themselves a little break. I was fit, but I picked myself apart and focused on the negative things about my body, not the positive. We always judge ourselves, whether we're a supermodel or not. If I knew then how awesome and flat my stomach was, I would have gone easier on myself. I've had to accept, too, that without the use of my hands, I can't do my own hair. That is at the top of the list of things I wish I could do. Britney still comes over sometimes to help me with my hair. She lives close enough that she can do that, and I love that she'll stop by if I need her. I have figured out with the bending of my wrist how to grip cosmetics enough to actually do my own makeup. It wasn't easy to master, and some days I didn't look exactly like I wanted to, but now I'd say I do a pretty darn good job.

There are so many girl things that are impacted by this chair, such as my desire to be a mother. I face a lot of hurdles, such as weaning myself off certain meds. I have to do that gradually to get ready to have a baby, so that's hard. I am on pain meds that I don't want to be on when I am pregnant, but my main concern is the medication that keeps my blood pressure up. It constricts the veins, which isn't good when blood is trying to get to your baby.

© REVOLUTION STUDIOS OF NORTH CAROLINA

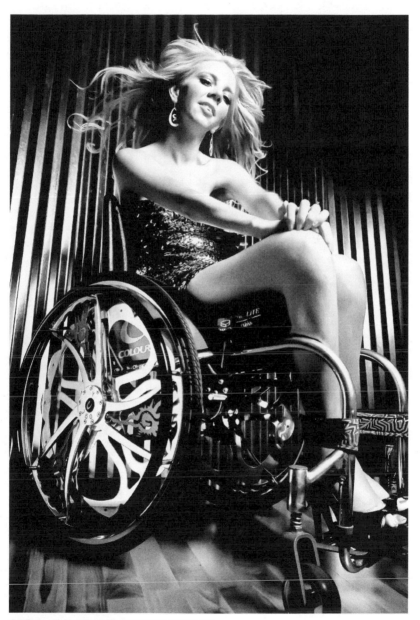

© REVOLUTION STUDIOS OF NORTH CAROLINA

© REVOLUTION STUDIOS OF NORTH CAROLINA

In the first two months of pregnancy, the veins need to open up even more. I already have low blood pressure, so imagine taking that medicine away. What might happen in those two months when my veins are open even more? It will be a major challenge. It's not this difficult with most spinal cord injuries. I have added health issues, and therefore I have to find doctors who specialize in my situation. Even though I am struggling with doctors' bills, I know my family and Chris's family will not let anything get in the way, because they want us to have this baby. They'll support us financially as best they can. Ideally, if I had $80,000, I could have someone else carry it. This would be the best option for me, and I so wish I had the finances to do it, but I don't. And I would never ask a friend to be our carrier. I don't want anyone to offer out of guilt. It's not something anyone I know would be interested in, and I would never put them on the spot like that.

I am afraid of getting pregnant: It's not bad for the baby, but it's bad for me. I think my lifestyle change will be dramatic. I won't move for months. I may be in bed for months, because I likely won't be able to sit up due to my low blood pressure. When I'm lying down my blood pressure is higher. Sometimes I can't sit up or I'll feel like I'm going to pass out. It happens to me now. I have that feeling, and then I just take my meds and lie down and wait for them to kick in. Then I'm usually okay. If I'm not on the medication, as long as I'm lying down, I won't pass out. Still, even though it would be nine months of hell, this is something I really, really want and something Chris wants, too. I'm not willing to give that up just to avoid being bedridden for a few months out of my entire life.

The hurdle right now isn't the fear of being in bed; it's the fear of getting off of my medication. I want a baby now. I wanted it yesterday. But I have to get over that mental block and get off the meds. I've had an initial conversation with the doctor and I'm on prenatal pills, which I need to take for six months. So we're prepping. We're a year away from trying.

I used to want one boy and one girl, but I'll probably be able to have only one child. I think pregnancy will be hard on my body, so one will be it for me. And that's okay. Financially, it will likely be out of reach for us to have more than one. Everyone in my family knows how important this is for us, and they're going to do everything in their power to help us through.

My girlfriends are so excited. They have told me they are ready to be aunts and to help spoil my child. I think they're not quite ready to be mothers themselves, so this will be fun for them, too. They've all expressed a lot of concern over the way in which I'll have to exist during the pregnancy, the pain and being stationary, but I think that with them around, I'll get through it. I know they're excited because they pretty regularly say, "What's the status of our niece or nephew?"

Lauren comes from a big family and we've talked a lot about kids, but she's just not ready yet to have a baby. I'm thinking I'll be the first one of our little group. I'm ready to get started. But she will eventually have children, and we both know it will be fun when we can share that experience. I hope our kids are close friends the way she and I are. I hope all of our kids maintain the bond we all have with each other.

◆～

It was an exhilarating feeling being pushed by the ocean like that. I felt free and strong as the wave caught me and carried me to shore. I had never surfed before the accident, just bodyboarded.

The feeling was similar. But this time, it felt like more of an accomplishment for me.

People ask me all the time if I'm afraid to go swimming or if I'm afraid of pools or the water in general. I get cold so easily now, so the water has to be really warm for me to go in, like the ocean on a hot summer day, or a therapy pool. But afraid? I'm not afraid at all. There's really nothing to be afraid of. I'm not afraid of what lies ahead for my life. I carry no grudges and no blame. I have no fear or anger toward the pool. It's not the pool's fault or the water's fault or her fault. It's one of those things that was no one's fault. I don't blame the water or the floor of the pool, and I certainly don't blame her. It's also pretty clearly not going to happen again. So, despite it all, I still love the water. I grew up by the water.

I can still feel water on my shoulders and my face when I'm submerged, and there's a space on the inside of my arms where I can feel it, too. Instead of dwelling on what I can't feel, I concentrate on what I can feel, the places where I do feel the touch of water. It's not weird to me anymore, the way it was that night in the pool or when I first showered in rehab, where the water was dripping down from a shower but I couldn't feel it. I'm so aware and appreciative of the little things that I can feel—the water on my neck, or my wet hair. I love the feeling of the water, the ocean, and the sand. I love it all, still.

Surfing was a dream come true for me. Life got harder for me, but my life is not over. Still, I'd rather surf standing up. I have a list of things I dream of doing one day if a cure ever becomes a reality in my lifetime, things I probably took for granted before the accident. Chris once said it was hard to remember back to when we just walked out and got into the car. I'd give anything to do that again. That, and a lot of other things, too. They aren't extravagant adventures, but everyday things I barely thought about before the accident. I want to do a cartwheel again, throw a football, and play tennis. I want to bodysurf, dance in my husband's arms, and climb a tree. Someday, I hope to walk my dog, style my own hair, and do sit-ups.

Mostly, I dream that one day when Chris holds my hand, I will be able to hold his right back.

Acknowledgments

Putting it all out there in this book has been both cathartic and challenging. I thank you all for reading my story, here and throughout the years in the news following my accident. So many of you reached out with kindness, without which I would never have gotten through this, so thank you for all of the letters, e-mails, encouragement, and generous donations.

I'd like to thank my agent, Maura Teitelbaum, for believing in my story; my editor, Lara Asher at GPP, for the care she put into weaving it together; and my project editor, Lauren Brancato, for her final manuscript fixes.

Thank you to Stephanie Krikorian for helping me get the words out of my head and onto the page. I appreciate greatly the time and effort you spent on my life story.

From the bottom of my heart, I want to thank my mom, Carol Friedman. Without hesitation, you left your life to help me live mine in the most normal way possible. Thank you for being my best friend. A huge thank you to my dad, Larry Friedman. You've always worked your butt off for this family. Thanks for teaching me to be a fighter.

And to Chris's parents, Susan and Bob Chapman, who have helped us stay afloat in hard times on more than one occasion: You have been a second set of parents to me, and I'm so grateful to have you both as my in-laws.

To my brother, Aaron Friedman: You have been such a big help, and I love you very much.

To Tom Vrnak: You've been such a good friend to me and Chris. Thank you for staying with me in the ICU so my mom and Chris could sleep that one night, for being our best man, and for being a night owl like me, so I have someone to talk to when I can't sleep.

If I haven't said it enough, to you four girls who shared that night by the pool with me, I love you and will always. You all stuck with me through hard times when many people walked away. The love, support, and loyalty that was always a part of our friendships was solidified on that spring night.

I'd like to thank all of my sponsors and supporters and those organizations that have donated their services, products, and time so that I can live a happier, more independent life. They include BraunAbility, 1-800-Registry, Colours Wheelchair, Van Products, Toyota, *George to the Rescue*, Lulus.com, Home Builders Association of Raleigh-Wake County, *Today*, Martha Manning Photography, Erin McLean Events, Morse Entertainment, Made-Up Special Events, New Mobility Resource, PhotoAbility, Crossfit APx, Drive Medical, Ocean Cure, and Walking with Anthony.

Of course, the love of my life, Chris Chapman, we have something so special that no one can ever break. I can't wait to celebrate My Bucket Got a Hole in It Day year in and year out for the rest of our lives. I'll continue to rub your back every night before bed as long as you keep calling me your sweetheart.

To my alma mater, East Carolina University, and to the Pirate nation for all of your support, and of course, for being the place at which I met my man. Once a Pirate, always a Pirate.

Reading Group Guide

1. What do you think of the Prologue and the way Rachelle describes the feeling of being stuck? How do you think the analogy of the "pause button" does or does not have relevance in her life after the accident?

2. In the first paragraph of Chapter 1, Rachelle talks about how carefully she and Chris planned out their future. How does this foreshadow the events to come? In what ways do they achieve or not achieve their goals?

3. What do you think of how Rachelle and Chris met? Do you think their initial friendship is what ultimately made their relationship so strong? Is your significant other also your best friend?

4. It can be fun to get all dolled up and find that perfect pair of shoes for a special occasion. On page 9, before her bachelorette party, Rachelle says, "I wanted the perfect white high heels, or else I felt like the entire outfit would be ruined." Does this statement seem insignificant now? Have you ever had a time in your life when you worried about something somewhat superficial only to later realize how unimportant it was?

5. The night of the accident the girls form a silent pact, an unbreakable bond, among them. Do you have a group of friends that you have this type of powerful bond with? Have you experienced any moments of tragedy in which you have helped one another survive, either physically or emotionally?

6. What are some of the things we take for granted in our day-to-day lives? After Rachelle's accident she can no longer hold Chris's hand or do her own hair. Are there ways to feel more gratitude for the seemingly little things in life?

7. In Chapter 8 Rachelle talks about how she wasn't able to cry and was finding humor in her day-to-day moments. What do you think about others' expectations of how we should react in moments of challenge or tragedy? Do you find it strange that she didn't cry or get angry? Do you think it's interesting that her honest, true reaction was so different from what others assumed it would be? What can you learn from this?

8. In Chapter 9, when Rachelle chronicles her experiences in rehab, she talks about how her friend Carly even learned to insert her catheter. On page 57 she says, "I think we women, as a group, underestimate our power." Do you agree? Can you share any memories you have of the collective power of women?

9. In Chapter 10, on page 60, Rachelle mentions that many people asked if she and Chris would still be together after the accident; she feels sorry for them because they must not know true love. Do you think their question is a valid one? If you were in a similar situation, would you have to think about it or would it never even cross your mind?

10. Do you believe everything happens for a reason? In Chapter 10 Rachelle talks about this statement and the idea that other people had that positive thinking could lead to her walking again. Do you think this belief is more harmful or helpful to people? Are there times when it's appropriate and times when it isn't?

11. In Chapter 12 Rachelle takes her first trip outside of the hospital and visits a park where she has an "able-bodied" history. Can you imagine how that would be difficult? Have you ever been in a situation where you return to a place that is full of memories of another time? Her father makes the profound statement, "It's actually a really good and important philosophy to make new memories every single day, especially now that you are healing. We shouldn't live for old ones. We should live for new ones." What do you think of this? Why is it important? How can you apply it to your own life?

12. In Chapter 13 Rachelle describes having sex with Chris for the first time after the accident. Do you think the intimacy between them has grown? How does Rachelle find other ways to feel connected to Chris? What do you find more important, physical or emotional intimacy?

13. How do you think Rachelle's competitive spirit helps her to recover from the accident? How does seeing her rehab as a game help her to get through it? How much does attitude have to do with it? She talks about the difference between her father, who never simply let her win, and kids today, who are more coddled in that respect. Do you think that it means more when you have to work for something? Are we doing a disservice to today's kids by giving them all trophies? Does hard work build resilience in the long run?

14. When Rachelle comes home from rehab, her mother has to move in with her to help care for her. How would you feel if your mother moved in with you? Would it be difficult? How might it change the nature of your bond?

15. What do you think about some of the issues Rachelle now faces, such as parking? Are you surprised by how thoughtless people can be? Are there ways we can change this behavior by enforcing stricter laws and/or higher fines?

16. What do you think of the pact that the five friends made? In today's world of posting everything on Facebook and Twitter, do you think it shows a strong sense of character that these women were able to keep this important secret? What do you think of the word *prank?* Was it mean of the media to use such a word? Does the Internet provide a forum where people can more easily hide behind their cruelty?

17. In Chapter 20 Rachelle talks about turning down Oprah and how her concern grew for the friend who had playfully pushed her. She tells the friend not to waste her money paying someone for help because Rachelle will always be there to listen. What do you think of this? Would you have suggested that your friend see a professional therapist?

18. What do you think of Rachelle's friend Sandra? Do you think it would be hard to be left out of the group that made the pact after the accident, or do you think in some ways she's lucky she wasn't there? Were her reaction and behavior immature? Do you think you can have a real friendship with someone who doesn't make the effort to spend time with you during a challenging time? Have you had any moments in your life where you feel as if you found out who your true friends were?

19. Do you think that Rachelle and Chris's wedding was more meaningful in some ways because of everything they had been through? Was it a milestone for everyone? Did it provide a sense of closure after such a terrible tragedy?

20. In Chapter 34 Rachelle talks about whether she'd rather bear her friend's burden or her own. Which do you think would be harder?

21. What do you think of the water imagery in the Epilogue? Are you surprised that Rachelle still has no fear of the water and in fact loves it? Are you impressed by her courage to try surfing?

22. What do you think of Rachelle's comments in the Epilogue about how women are always judging themselves and picking themselves apart? Do you find yourself doing that, too? After reading her story, can you better accept your physical appearance and appreciate all that your body can do for you?

About the Author

Rachelle Friedman, once a program assistant at a seniors activity center who taught aerobics and line dancing in North Carolina, is still recovering from an accident on the night of her bachelorette party that left her paralyzed from the chest down. She spends her time as an advocate for others with spinal cord injuries and is hoping to pursue a new career one day soon. She makes daily efforts through speaking engagements and social media to inspire people with her optimism and her bright and vibrant spirit. Rachelle grew up loving the ocean, cheerleading in high school, and playing sports. Although she tackles physical activities a little differently now, Rachelle still surfs, plays rugby on an otherwise all-male team, and loves the outdoors. She recently learned to drive on her own and is working at perfecting her skills on the road. Rachelle has appeared on most major news outlets in the United States and has been and is still being written about in thousands of publications worldwide. Rachelle graduated from East Carolina University, majoring in sports recreation. She and her husband, Chris Chapman, live in Knightdale, North Carolina, with their two dogs. Visit her at rachellefriedman.com.